The New Americans
Recent Immigration and American Society

Edited by
Steven J. Gold and Rubén G. Rumbaut

A Series from LFB Scholarly

Immigration and Crime
The Effects of Immigration on Criminal Behavior

Jacob I. Stowell

LFB Scholarly Publishing LLC
New York 2007

Library of Congress Cataloging-in-Publication Data

Stowell, Jacob I., 1973-
  Immigration and crime : the effects of immigration on criminal
behavior / Jacob I. Stowell.
    p. cm. -- (The new Americans)
  Includes bibliographical references and index.
  ISBN-13: 978-1-59332-204-5 (alk. paper)
  1. Violent crime--Sociological aspects--United States--Research. 2.
United States--Emigration and immigration--Research. 3. Immigrants--
United States--Social conditions--Research. 4. Emigration and
immigration--Social aspects--Research. 5. Alien criminals--United
States--Research. I. Title.
  HV6181.S76 2007
  364.3086'9120973--dc22

2007014423

ISBN-10: 1-59332-204-6 (cloth)
ISBN-13: 978-1-59332-204-5

Printed on acid-free 250-year-life paper.

Manufactured in the United States of America.

Table of Contents

1149123

Acknowledgements

I am grateful and indebted to the many scholars and friends who made the completion of this work possible. The strong academic environment I experienced while at the University at Albany was instrumental in my development as a scholar. In particular, I would like to thank Dr. Steven Messner for his insightful comments on early drafts of this manuscript. This work was also funded, in part, by a research fellowship I received from the National Consortium on Violence Research (NCOVR). In addition to financial support, the fellowship afforded me the opportunity to work directly with Dr. Ramiro Martinez, Jr. Not only does this study build directly on the immigration research program initiated by Dr. Martinez, but his work continues to influence my current research projects. More importantly, Dr. Martinez has been an excellent mentor and I value his friendship both personally and professionally.

I would also like to thank the series editors Stephen J. Gold and Ruben G. Rumbaut for taking the time to review this manuscript. Finally, I would like to express my gratitude to Leo Balk at LFB Scholarly for providing me the opportunity to publish this work as a book.

CHAPTER 1

Introduction:

Reconsidering the Link Between Immigration and Crime

The goal of this research is to examine the impact of immigration on levels of violent crime. Specifically, this is a study of the extent to which the relative size of the foreign-born population is associated with violence. Using a combination of US Census data and tract-level crime data collected from official police department records, this research tests whether patterns of violent offending across neighborhoods (i.e., census tracts) are partially attributable to the population characteristics of an area, and particularly to its nativity composition.

The introductory chapter is designed to situate this research within a broad theoretical context that will provide insight into some of the key questions addressed by this study. Relevant to this discussion, it is important to highlight the unique contributions this research makes to our current understanding of the relationship between immigration and crime. Further, it is also important at the outset to describe the implications of immigration research, with respect to both current socio-demographic trends and ongoing public policy debates. Before moving into the more detailed aspects of this study, it will be instructive to review broadly the conceptual and theoretical perspectives informing this study.

Theoretical Framework

Criminological theories provide ample reason to expect that immigration and violent crime are causally related. For nearly a century, scholars have accepted the notion that immigration has a positive impact on levels of violent crime. In particular, social disorganization theory details how the arrival of immigrants undermines a community's ability to exercise effective social control over its residents.

Social disorganization theory is based on the urban ecological tradition advanced by researchers at the University of Chicago nearly a

1

century ago. Urban ecologists associated with the "Chicago School" argue that urban processes are governed by the laws of nature. Borrowing from the language of anatomy and evolutionary biology, scholars from the Chicago School describe cities as units constantly undergoing a process of "metabolism" in an ongoing effort to reach a state of "functional equilibrium" (Wirth 1938, Burgess 1925, Park 1936). It was through this process of urban redefinition (or reorganization) that places "sift and sort and relocate individuals and groups by residence and occupation" (Burgess 1925, p. 54). The sorting of residents, according to the ecological tradition, is the necessary outcome of urban growth and the city's attempt to accommodate increases in population, as well as to "maximize" its land use.

In the seminal book *Juvenile Delinquency and Urban Areas* Shaw and McKay (1969 [1942]) explain the high levels of crime in the urban neighborhoods using an ecological approach. Shaw and McKay argue that structural characteristics of urban neighborhoods make them particularly conducive to the commission of delinquent and criminal acts. Specifically, because urban communities experience "successive changes in [their] nativity and nationality composition," they are unable to exercise effective social controls over their members (Shaw and McKay 1969 [1942], p. 315). Lacking the necessary controls, socially disorganized neighborhoods will have increased levels of crime. Shaw and McKay (1969 [1942]: 315) also point out that despite the demographic turnover, these urban areas are characterized by high, "relatively constant" rates of delinquency.

Of particular interest to this study is the fact that social disorganization theory identifies immigration as a neighborhood characteristic associated with crime. Advocates of this perspective describe immigration as an inherently destabilizing, or disorganizing urban process. The ecological perspective posits that, because immigrants typically arrive in the United States lacking the qualities which would enable them to compete effectively for both occupational and residential opportunities, they are "sorted" into resource-poor neighborhoods, contributing to an area's level of economic deprivation.

In addition to promoting economic disadvantage, social disorganization theory argues that a continuous influx of immigrants increases levels of residential instability and demographic heterogeneity, both factors thought to undermine a community's ability to exercise effective social control over its residents. Ecologists argue that the high levels of criminal and non-criminal deviance in disorganized areas are not reflective of innate characteristics of their inhabitants, or subcultural belief systems. Rather, the increased prevalence of crime is the result of disrupted neighborhood social structure. However, the urban ecological perspective argues that areas with large immigrant populations frequently become havens of "crime and vice...free spirits...[and] disorderly life" (Burgess 1925; p. 38).

Social disorganization theory makes specific arguments as to the types of neighborhoods we would expect to have high rates of crime; namely, those that are poor, residentially unstable, and racially mixed. As described above, the logic underpinning social disorganization theory suggests that immigration contributes to each of the three factors associated with neighborhood disorder. In particular, disorganization theorists highlight the diversity of an area's immigrant population as playing a key role in its degree of social dislocation. Because of its deleterious impact on neighborhood structure, social disorganization theory presupposes a positive relationship between immigration and crime.

Although Shaw and McKay do not discuss their theoretical model in causal terms, there is no clear mention of crime as a necessary (direct) consequence of immigration. However, the logic of the theory implies that an indirect relationship exists. Consistent with the foundations of urban ecology, social disorganization theory argues that disorder is fueled by exogenous social forces, such as industrialization and immigration. The structural balance of an area is "disturbed" by an inability to adapt successfully to external pressures. In other words, external forces are viewed as the factors that set the process of social disorganization in motion (or maintain it). The theory does not view immigration as a cause of disorganization *per se*, but rather recognizes that immigration influences crime through its impact on the social structural characteristics of the areas into which immigrants settle.

The conceptual causal model implied by social disorganization theory is depicted in Figure 1.1. From this causal diagram, a more refined set of hypotheses regarding immigration and its potentially negative impacts on community social structure can be derived. As anticipated by the above discussion, this model indicates that social disorganization theory predicts a positive relationship between immigration and each of the structural dimensions Shaw and McKay (1969 [1942]) present as the causes of social disruption. Furthermore, it is clear in Figure 1.1 that the theory expects that each of the three structural sources of social disorganization, and not immigration, will have a direct, positive impact on levels of criminal behavior.

Figure 1.1. Indirect Causal Model Implied by Social Disorganization Theory.

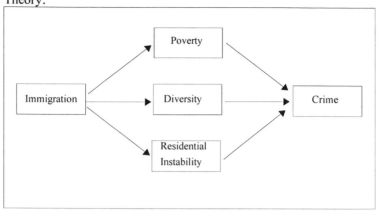

Although the theory draws a clear causal link between disorder and crime, a question remains regarding the consistency of immigration's impact on the social structural characteristics of an area. That is, the theory is less clear about whether the characteristics of an area's immigrant population may have varied impacts on social structure, and by extension, levels of violent offending. Implicit in the model is the notion that immigrants comprise a unified group, ignoring the possibility that there may be differences among an immigrant population that will be associated with differential impacts on the structural arrangement of an area. Rather than a consistent relationship between immigration and disorder, it may be that there are certain qualities about an immigrant population (e.g., length of time spent in the US, ethnicity) that are more likely to be related to higher levels of disorganization, and by consequence, increased levels of violent crime.

More generally, there are reasons to question whether the association between immigrant and crime operates as described by the theory. If an immigrant/crime link exists, it follows that 1) violent crime rates in largely immigrant communities would tend to be higher than in similarly situated non-immigrant neighborhoods; and 2) because of the large increase in immigrants over the past decade, violent crime rates should have also increased. Although research has yet to clarify the former point, *prima facie* evidence does not lend support to the latter. According to the Bureau of Justice Statistics, continuing a decade-long decline, national violent victimization rates reached an all-time low in 2002. Further, the overall decrease in violent crime is not attributable to large declines in one particular type of offending, as the rates of homicide, rape, robbery and assault have all experienced substantial reductions.[1] It is worth emphasizing the point that at the same time violent crime rates were falling, immigration to the US was thriving. Since 1990, the size of foreign-born population grew by 56%, an addition of nearly 11 million individuals.[2]

Recent scholarship also questions whether immigration is related to increased levels of violent crime (Martinez and Lee 2000a; Martinez 2002; Lee 2003; Lee and Martinez 2002; Hagan and Palloni 1998). Martinez and colleagues consistently find little empirical support for the immigrant/crime link. As Martinez and Lee (2000a: 486) argue, "in many cases, compared with native groups, immigrants seem better able to withstand crime-facilitating [neighborhood] conditions than native groups." Although the body of immigration/crime research is growing, Martinez and Lee (2000a: 486) maintain that additional research is necessary before the question of whether "immigrant groups faced with adverse social conditions maintain low rates of crime" can be answered definitively.

The findings reported in the contemporary immigration/crime literature are interesting because there are no clear theoretical reasons to expect a direct relationship between immigration and crime. Nowhere in Shaw and McKay's original theoretical formulation is there mention of how exogenous factors such as immigration may directly influence levels of criminal behavior. That is to say, according to the conceptual model presented in Figure 1.1, social disorganization theory does not discuss the possibility that immigration may have both direct and indirect effects on crime. Moreover, with its focus on the strong impacts of external social forces on crime, the reported *negative* relationship seems inconsistent with the underlying theoretical rationale.

Although not discussed by social disorganization theorists, more recent research on immigration provides some insight into why a negative relationship between immigration and crime might be expected (see Kao and Tienda 1995; Ogbu 1991; Model 1995; Zhang and Sanders 1999). For example, selectivity theory argues that immigrants who decide to come to America do so for the opportunity to improve their life chances. Central to the selectivity theory is the belief

---

1   Bureau of Justice Statistics (http://www.ojp.usdoj.gov/bjs).
2   (http://factfinder.census.gov/home/saff/main.html?_lang=en).

that "persons who migrate are more ambitious, talented, and diligent than those who do not" (Model 1995: 538). The selectivity theory would expect that because most immigrants are "hard-working [and] ready to defer gratification in the interest of long-term advancement" they are less likely to engage in criminal behavior (Tonry 1997: 21).

Another explanation advanced by immigration scholars is the "immigrant optimism" hypothesis (Kao and Tienda 1995; Ogbu 1991; Chiswick 1979; Zhou and Bankston 1998; Zhang and Sanders 1999; Portes 1996; Waters 1999; Portes and Rumbaut 2001). The immigrant optimism hypothesis posits that despite the hardship and socioeconomic disadvantages, immigrants remain committed to their aspirations of conventional success because they believe they have more opportunities in the US than were available in their countries of origin. As Kao and Tienda (1995: 5) argue, in part because immigrants often "faced harsher environments [in their home countries]...they are more creative in inventing pragmatic solutions to their current predicaments." The implication of the optimism hypothesis is that immigrant populations, due to their orientation towards conventional achievement, are likely to be associated with reduced levels of criminal behavior.

Figure 1.2. Direct and Indirect Effects of Immigration on Crime.

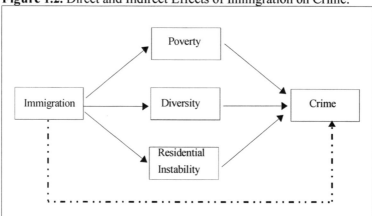

Both the immigrant optimism and selectivity hypotheses offer theoretical reasons for expecting a direct negative effect of immigration on crime. However, such a relationship implies a different causal structure than that first offered by Shaw and McKay (see Figure 1.2). According to the revised theoretical model presented in Figure 1.2, understanding the overall relationship between immigration and crime requires considering both its relationship to crime directly, as well as its impact on the social structural characteristics of an area. Studies that examine both types of causal relationships are lacking among recent criminological research on immigration, which focuses primarily on the direct effects (Martinez 2002; Lee 2003; Martinez and Lee 2000a; Lee et al. 2001; Lee and Martinez 2002). By not considering both causal mechanisms, current research does not yield a complete picture of the ways in which immigration may be related to crime.

The current study stems directly from the contemporary line of research, which seeks to test empirically the immigrant/crime link. However, the present study expands on this tradition by addressing some of the limitations of prior research. First, I make use of exploratory spatial data analytical (ESDA) techniques to inspect whether immigrants and violent crime concentrate spatially. Second, this study employs analytical models that are more consistent with social disorganization theory. The theoretically informed empirical models provide a more detailed view of both the direct and indirect effects of immigration on levels of violent crime. Finally, this study broadens the scope of immigration/crime scholarship by predicting the impact of immigration on a wider array of violent crimes than are used in most current studies. Each of the contributions will be discussed in greater detail in the following section.

Research Contributions

One contribution of this research is the specific focus on the purported relationship between immigration and crime. Interestingly, the early work of urban scholars and criminologists focused on the impacts of immigration on their receiving communities. Although the topic has remained an important one to many contemporary urban scholars, this is less true for crime researchers. Disproportionately, the discussions of crime are concerned with explaining the differences in the levels of "black and white" offending/victimization (see Martinez 2002). The need for more criminological investigations paying special attention to immigration is particularly important given the tremendous increase in the size of the immigrant population, particularly over the past decade. Therefore, a goal of this study is to cast new light on a discussion that began over a century ago, but which has largely fallen out of the purview of contemporary criminological research.

A substantive contribution of this study is that it examines both the direct and indirect effects of immigration on crime. Unlike prior studies, this research is sensitive to the notion that both causal processes may be operating simultaneously. Indeed, there are theoretical reasons to expect the direct negative association between immigration and crime that is commonly reported in the contemporary immigration/crime studies (Martinez and Lee 1998, 2000a; Lee 2003; Nielsen et al. 2005). However, I argue that using immigration only as a predictor of crime, ignores a theoretically important aspect of social disorganization theory; namely, the influence of immigration on social structure. A central tenet of the disorganization perspective is the notion that exogenous factors such as immigration have an impact on crime through their negative impacts on structure. Examining both causal mechanisms within a single analytical framework offers a fresh perspective on the interrelationship between immigration and criminal violence.

The current study extends beyond prior research in that it examines the immigrant/crime link using multiple dimensions of a neighborhood's foreign-born population, rather than the more general measures that have been employed in previous research. Consistent with social disorganization theory, there are reasons to expect that the influence of immigration on the social structural characteristics of an area is not uniform. For example, the ecological perspective argues that newly arrived immigrants are "sorted" into disorganized neighborhoods precisely because of their deficits in human and social capital. The recent immigrants also contribute to levels of disorganization by increasing overall levels of poverty and residential instability. As the skills and training necessary for conventional success are acquired over time, however, many immigrants will relocate to more socially organized neighborhoods. According to this ecological argument, social disorganization theory would expect areas comprised primarily of an older immigrant populations to be more structurally stable, and thus, have lower levels of violent crime.

National origin, or ethnicity, is another characteristic of the immigrant population that may be associated differentially with neighborhood violence. Introducing measures ethnicity to criminological studies of immigration represents an advancement over prior research, which focuses primarily on the impacts of overall levels of immigration on violence (Martinez and Lee 2000a; Lee 2003; Lee et al 2001). Summary indicators of immigration are informative because they offer broad insight into the hypothesized relationship between immigration and crime. Further, because the disorganization perspective makes general arguments regarding the impacts of immigration on criminal behavior, the treatment of immigrants as a unified group adheres to the theoretical logic. However, such measures are limited because they assume that the effects on crime are consistent across the foreign-born population. In other words, the measures of immigration typically included in quantitative analyses do not allow researchers to examine the degree to which levels of violence are associated with the presence of different immigrant groups.

The size and the racial and ethnic diversity of the current wave of immigration indicate the need for researchers to move beyond the conceptualization of immigrants as a single category (see Kleniewski 1997: Reid et al. 2005; Rumbaut et al. 2006). In addition to pointing out the high degree of demographic diversity, recent immigration research further illustrates the importance of including more refined measures of immigration. For example, Alba et al. (1999: 448) find that beyond the demographic differences, the current immigration stream "encompasses a wide spectrum of human capital." Because immigrant groups arrive in the United States with differences in levels of educational or occupational training, it may be that these disparities are linked to different opportunity structures. Those who arrive with higher levels of capital will have an increased probability of upward social mobility through conventional channels. More generally, the current immigration scholarship illustrates the need for crime researchers to be more sensitive to variations within the immigrant population.

The implication of this finding for the current study is that, contrary to theoretical expectations, immigration may not have a uniform impact on violence. If members of a particular ethnic group tend to arrive with marketable job skills, there is no reason to expect that their presence will be associated with high levels of violence. The same can be said for immigrants who arrive with lower levels of capital, but who belong to groups who have established strong kinship and employment networks. Individuals in the latter case may be more likely to be channeled into immigrant neighborhoods where they will have both filial ties to the community as well as opportunities to work, and thus, experience a smoother transition into conventional life in

American society. By analyzing the degree to which immigrant ethnicity influences violence differently, this study sheds new light on a component of the immigrant/crime relationship that criminologists have yet to explore.

The research undertaken in this project expands on previous immigration/crime research by introducing multiple indicators of violent crime. The majority of empirical research on this issue focuses exclusively on the association between immigration and homicide (Martinez 2002; Martinez and Lee 2000a; Lee 2003; Lee et al. 2001; Lee and Martinez 2002). The scholarship of Martinez and colleagues offers little support for the hypothesized immigrant/crime link. Indeed, often levels of homicide are significantly *lower* than would be expected considering the structural disadvantage experienced in the typical neighborhoods under investigation. Clearly, using homicide as the primary measure of violence provides evidence contrary to the popular beliefs regarding the relationship between immigration and crime. A question that remains is whether this pattern holds for other forms of violent crime.

To address this question, this study investigates the immigrant/crime link using measures of crime that include both lethal and non-lethal expressions of violence. Using additional indicators of violence represents an undeveloped research area and one that contributes to our current knowledge regarding the association between immigration and crime. The social disorganization theory does not explicate whether particular types of crime are more likely to characterize disrupted areas. Some researchers hypothesize that immigration is more likely to be associated with instrumental (i.e., property-based offenses) rather than expressive crimes (i.e., violent offenses not involving property) (see Hagan and Palloni 1999). However, empirical research has yet to substantiate this argument. If this research reveals that different causal patterns emerge for different types of violent behavior, this finding will have implications for both public policy considerations and future research designed to test social disorganization theory. Furthermore, testing the theory using only one type of crime may mask larger patterns, and therefore, the results may overstate the lack of quantitative support for the social disorganization perspective.

A final contribution this research makes is that it considers the spatial distributions of immigrants and violent crime. The social disorganization theory is underpinned by a strong argument regarding the spatial dispersion of crime. Indeed, Shaw and McKay (1969

[1942]) used a series of maps to support their claim that a preponderance of officially recorded criminal behavior is concentrated within particular portions of an urban area. Following in this tradition, I use current mapping and spatial analytic techniques, which allow me to test statistically the degree to which immigration and violent crime are geographically concentrated. Although mapping is common in the recent research on immigration and crime, the use of advanced spatial analytic tools has yet to be introduced as an initial test of the geographic arguments guiding the social disorganization perspective.

Research Implications

Just as it was an important research topic at the beginning of the last century, immigration is a topic receiving much attention from contemporary academics. With current rates of immigration rivaling those of a century ago, it appears that the United States is experiencing another "great wave" of immigration. During the first two decades of the twentieth century, the size of the foreign-born population grew by thirty-five percent, an increase of over 3.5 million individuals. In absolute terms, this meant that the size of the foreign-born population increased to nearly 14 million (14.2 percent of the total population).[3] Rates of immigration ebbed in the middle of the last century, but are once again on the rise (Kleniewski 1997; US Census Bureau 2000). In 1970, immigrants comprised less than 5 percent of the total US population, but this number more than doubled over the next three decades. By 2000 immigrants comprised over 11 percent of the total population (US Census Bureau 2000). The growth in the number of immigrants has accelerated particularly over the past decade, during which time the size of the immigrant population increased by nearly 60 percent, now totaling more than 31 million persons.

Unlike the earlier waves of immigration, the current influx of immigrants is not predominantly of European heritage (Kleniewski 1997; Butcher and Piehl 1998a; Massey 1995). The observed increase is primarily attributable to the growth in the Hispanic population, which increased by roughly 80 percent over the past decade, an expansion of over six million persons. Over the same period, the number of foreign-born Asians more than doubled, increasing in size by 2.5 million individuals.[4] These large population shifts are bound to have

---

3   http://www.census.gov/population/www/documentation/twps0029/tab01.htm.
4   1990 and 2000 population counts provided by US Census STF 4a and SF3.

implications for the host society, many of which are yet to be quantified. Included in that list is the impact that the rise in immigration has had on violent crime rates.

In addition to its impact on the social and economic structure of American society, the rapid increase in foreign-born individuals also influences public perceptions of immigration. To address this issue, the 1994 General Social Survey (GSS), a nationally representative sample of American adults, included a special module on immigration. From these data a clear pattern regarding the perceived socially disruptive impact of immigration emerges (see Davis and Smith 1999). Specifically, nearly two-thirds (64%) of the survey respondents report that they believe immigrants make it difficult to keep the country united. At the national level, these data show the general concern over the disorganizing effects of immigration.

The negative public perceptions of immigration also color views regarding the interrelationship between immigration and crime. Empirical evidence suggests that the belief that immigration and crime are inextricably linked continues to be strongly held in the public consciousness. In part this is driven by the provincial concerns in areas where the size of the foreign-born population is growing rapidly. For example, Gonzales (1996) argues that the renewed interest in deporting illegal immigrants in San Diego was informed more by the popular concern over the burden that "criminal aliens" were having on the criminal justice system rather than by actual arrest statistics. National trends mirror this local sentiment, as the 1996 GSS reports that over thirty percent of the respondents believed that immigrants caused increases in crime. It is important to note that these beliefs are not supported by academic research. The disparity between public perceptions of immigration and the results reported in the immigrant/crime literature suggest the need for additional research on this topic.

The analyses contained in this study are designed with that goal in mind; namely, to incorporate alternative theoretical and methodological approaches in an effort to understand more completely the relationship between immigration and crime within a contemporary social context. Although research on this topic began nearly a century ago, questions regarding the overall impact of immigration on crime remain. Recent scholarship suggests that immigration may have a suppressive influence on levels of criminal behavior. Although these findings stand in contrast to the claims made by social disorganization theory, there are also theoretical reasons to consider additional causal mechanisms.

However, the analytical techniques typically used in existing studies make it difficult to assess whether the observed countervailing effect will emerge after partialling out the effect of immigration on social structure. It is hoped that the findings of this study will contribute to ongoing discussions regarding the immigrant/crime link by informing both policy debates and future academic investigations.

CHAPTER 2

Social Disorganization Theory:
Expectations and Empirical Realities

The notion that immigration and crime are inextricably linked is not a new one. This relationship has been the topic of academic discussions for over a century. For example, in a study of patterns of arrest in Philadelphia, Sanderson (1856) reports that although there was variation between ethnic groups, immigrant arrest rates were nearly ten times higher than those of native-born individuals. The belief that immigrants have higher criminogenic tendencies filtered into the public consciousness and has been used to fuel nationalistic/isolationist rhetoric and anti-immigration movements (see Lamm and Imhoff 1985; see also Martinez 2002). The same argument regarding the immigration/crime link is still commonly used by immigration opponents (Brimelow 1996, Gurr 1989; Lamm and Imhoff 1985). As Gurr (1989, p. 76) argues "America's three great crime waves can be linked to immigration...[and that] episodes of violent crime wound down as immigrants were incorporated into the expanding economy."[5] However, because his empirical findings consistently fail to find support for this relationship, Martinez (2002) concludes that the belief in the immigrant/crime link is perpetuated by negative media stereotypes.

Despite being the subject of a long-standing debate, surprisingly, there are relatively few quantitative studies that examine how immigration impacts neighborhood levels of violent crime. Criminological theories do provide a rationale for why we would expect immigration to be linked to increases in crime. In particular, social disorganization theory makes specific claims regarding the

---

5   Gurr (1989) and Brimelow (1996) argue that America's "three great crime waves" began in 1800, 1850, and 1960 each lasting between 20 and 30 years.

impact of immigration on the social structure of communities. This chapter outlines the social disorganization theoretical tradition including a discussion of the major contributions of this perspective and a review of the empirical tests of this theory.

Social Disorganization Theory

The social disorganization theory builds on a theoretical tradition that began at the University of Chicago. The Chicago School of sociology, and more specifically, its emphasis on urban ecology enjoyed disciplinary prominence for the first half of the twentieth century. Of primary interest to these researchers were the mechanisms through which urban areas were able to adapt to and reorganize in response to external social pressures. Because this was a time when the city of Chicago and its surrounding area were undergoing dramatic social redefinition, the setting provided an ideal social laboratory to test the ecological theory of urban change. To put the magnitude of the social change in perspective, during the first two decades of the twentieth century, the area's total population nearly doubled and by 1920 over 3.3 million people lived in the Chicago metropolitan region. During this same period, the size of the immigrant population more than tripled, totaling nearly one-third of the metropolitan region's total population by 1920.[6] The steep rise in overall population and particularly the increase in the number of immigrants raised questions regarding how cities adapted structurally to incorporate newcomers.

As mentioned previously, the theory of urban processes advanced by the Chicago School is based on the tradition of urban ecology. The ecological doctrine informing the Chicago School's explanation of urban processes is clearly evident in the Burgess' (1925) well-known concentric-zone model of Chicago. In this model, Burgess argues that a city is characterized by a series of successive zones, each identifiable by the characteristics of their population and how their land is utilized. Essentially, the zones centered around the city's central business district (CBD) and land values increased as areas become increasingly residential moving away from the CBD. According to this model, as the city expands, there is a "tendency of each inner zone to extend its area by the invasion of the next outer zone" (Burgess 1925, p. 50). Further, the theory posits that although urbanization disrupts

---

6   1900 and 1920 data are taken from IPUMS 5% sample files (see Ruggles et al. 2004).

community cohesion, the process ultimately facilitates optimal land use and social stability. In other words, through expansion and redefinition, a city is better able to address the needs of its residents. The ecological theory stipulates that competition determines how cities make best use of available land. As a city grows, struggles over place ensue between parties with various land use interests. Ecologists argue that the competition is primarily over land in the center of the cities, areas "destined to serve the whole metropolitan region" (Park 1936, p. 8). The interested party who wins the battle for place, according to the theory, is the one that is best suited to occupy a given location. In other words, this theory presupposes that the outcomes of such land use battles and the ability of a business to flourish in a given location are determined by the larger ecological needs of the city. Moreover, because urban areas are generally perceived as cohesive units, urban ecologists contend that through competition, individuals and businesses alike are "sorted" into their optimal locations. Simply put, whatever the outcomes of the competition, the results are seen as beneficial to the city as a whole because they contribute to a state of social balance, or equilibrium.

There is a clear functionalist orientation to the urban tradition associated with the Chicago School. Ecologists emphasize not only the role of competition, but also the importance of interdependency in establishing social equilibrium. Further, while ecologists perceive urban processes as part of an "orderly process of change and development" for the city as a whole, they recognize that urban processes carry with them negative consequences (Park 1936, p. 9). Urban ecologists do not perceive that all residents share equally in the benefits of the shifting and reorganization associated with urbanization. Rather, the ecological theorists are keenly aware that as a product of urbanization, there are large disparities in terms of the quality of the neighborhoods into which individuals and groups are "sorted." However, the theory proposes that the most disadvantaged areas of a city serve as temporary destinations for persons who are yet to acquire levels of social and human capital required for improved occupational and residential attainment.

The areas closest to the city center, or the "zone in transition," are the most likely to be characterized by high levels of poverty, residential instability, and racial/ethnic heterogeneity (Burgess 1925). Such neighborhoods are thought to be not only economically disadvantaged, but also socially "disorganized." A primary consequence of disorganization, ecologists argue, is that it renders certain areas unable to exercise effective social control over their residents. As Louis Wirth (1938: 8) argues, individuals living in urban settings and particularly those in distressed communities will experience difficulty establishing bonds to other individuals or to local institutions, which together form effective networks of social control. Lacking strong social control mechanisms, disorganized neighborhoods are also the ones with the highest levels of "crime and vice...free spirits...[and] disorderly life" (Burgess 1925, p. 38). What is interesting about the ecological perspective is that it focuses on community structure as a key to understanding the differential impacts of urban processes on neighborhood outcomes.

Moreover, urban ecologists perceive social fragmentation as a direct consequence of urban processes. Unlike contemporary urban scholars, proponents of this perspective are less critical of social isolation, arguing that "segregation offers the group, and thereby the individuals who compose the group, a place and a role in the total organization of city life" (Burgess 1925, p. 56; see also Hawley 1986). This is not to say that the urban ecologists are unaware of the negative impacts of the sorting process, as they note that the areas with socially isolated populations also tend to be those with the highest levels of disorganization. Ecologists recognize that in addition to being spatially concentrated, disorganized neighborhoods are also resource poor. This means that, coupled with a lack of effective mechanisms of informal social control, such areas also have the least ability to buffer the community against the negative consequences of disruption.

Shaw and McKay (1969 [1942]) ground social disorganization theory in the ecological tradition associated with the Chicago School. Adhering to the principles of urban ecology, Shaw and McKay argue that structural characteristics of particular urban neighborhoods, and not the characteristics of their residents, make them particularly conducive to the commission of delinquent acts. At a time when biological- or psychological-based theories of crime were not uncommon, social disorganization theory proposed that high rates of neighborhood crime were attributable to the structure of the communities, rather than the characteristics of their inhabitants. In other words, social disorganization theory explains crime by focusing on the characteristics of places, not people.

Social disorganization theory identifies three primary structural characteristics that can be used as proxies to gauge the extent to which an area is socially disrupted. Moreover, the theory argues that these characteristics are highly correlated with levels of crime. First, the theory posits that the economic deprivation of a community, generally thought of as area's poverty rate, is an important predictor of social disruption. A second condition is the degree of residential stability, which is conceptualized as the length of time individuals/families have lived in a given area. Social disorganization theory contends that high levels of population turnover, or instability, are common in disorganized areas. Finally, heterogeneity refers to the racial/ethnic composition of an area. The social disorganization perspective contends that a mixed racial/ethnic neighborhood composition, and more specifically, the corresponding language and/or cultural differences, inhibit social cohesion. Although these characteristics are discussed separately, disorganization theorists recognize that these conditions are likely to concentrate spatially. Therefore, although any one of the factors may be related to violent crime, it is their combination which increases the likelihood that higher levels of crime will characterize certain neighborhoods.

The theory indicates that the reason why such neighborhoods are prone to crime is because they are unable to exercise effective social control over their residents. Specifically, Shaw and McKay argue that a consequence of social disruption is that it undermines a community's sense of cohesion. In poor, ethnically mixed, and residentially unstable areas, it is increasingly difficult for their members to foster and maintain strong attachments to local institutions or other residents. Individuals living in such areas are more inclined to keep to themselves, less inclined to watch out for the neighborhood, and thus, less likely to intervene on behalf of the neighborhood when they witness the commission of crimes or other deviant behavior (see Sampson et al. 1997; Sampson and Raudenbush 1999). Lacking the necessary controls, the children (and adults) living in distressed areas are left to their own devices, which often leads to involvement in crime or other deviant activities. Further, social disorganization theory points out that increased rates of crime and other forms of deviant conduct become enduring characteristics of some urban communities.

The social control argument discussed above is the one most commonly associated with the work of Shaw and McKay. In reality, the authors offer another explanation for why crime flourishes in some neighborhoods. In *Juvenile Delinquency and Urban Areas,* the authors acknowledge that it is possible for crime to be the result of a concerted effort on the part of those living in disadvantaged areas to compensate for a lack of resources and blocked opportunities. The following passage illustrates the second explanatory model:

The differentiation of areas and the segregation of populations within the city have resulted in wide variation of opportunities in the struggle for position within the social order. The groups in the areas of lowest economic status find themselves at a disadvantage in the struggle to achieve the goals idealized in our civilization...and that the economic position of persons living in areas of least opportunity should be translated into unconventional conduct (quoted from Cullen and Agnew 1999, p. 69)

The quote above indicates that it is because opportunities for conventional success are in short supply that individuals are more likely to engage in criminal deviance. Further, this opportunity/motivational argument is reflected in many of the ethnographic accounts of crime that were written during the same period (see Thrasher 1963; Whyte 1955). Although the logic underpinning this explanation departs from the social control argument made earlier (see Kornhauser 1979), both theoretical positions assert that the origin of crime is rooted in neighborhood social structure.

The preceding review of the social disorganization perspective has highlighted the general tenets of the theory. It is important to note the particular attention disorganization theorists pay to what they perceive to be the disruptive force of immigration. Indeed, social disorganization theory contends that increased disorder, and by implication rates of crime, is especially likely during periods of large-scale immigration. Disorganization theorists argue that community formation is undermined by the increased language and cultural differences associated with a diverse immigrant population (see Thomas and Znaniecki 1920). Moreover, meaningful networks of monitoring and social control prove difficult to establish because the neighborhoods into which immigrant groups settle are often resource poor and residentially unstable. Thus, the theory speaks directly to why we would expect higher rates of violent crime in neighborhoods with large proportions of immigrants.

Contemporary Research on Social Disorganization Theory

Criminologists have used social disorganization theory as the foundation for countless research projects. Despite the support it has received in the empirical research literature, in recent years, scholars have called for a reinterpretation of the theory (Bursik 1984; Bursik and Grasmick 1992; Heitgard and Bursik 1987; Morenoff and Sampson 1997). In particular, the work of Robert Bursik and colleagues has pushed for a modification of the classical theoretical formulations. Some criminologists call into question the ecological/functionalist premises underpinning the theory (see Hagan 1994; Bursik 1989). For example, in his book *Crime and Disrepute,* Hagan (1994) recognizes that neighborhood disorganization results, in part, from a process of "disinvestment" whereby capital and resources are consciously and systematically channeled away from poor and minority neighborhoods (see also Wilson 1987). Similarly, Bursik (1989) argues that factors other than market-forces shape the ecological structure of communities. Thus, both Hagan and Bursik conclude that urban areas are not disrupted only as a consequence of unavoidable urban processes, but rather that this outcome is also a product of political decision making.

Interestingly, while Hagan's (1994) discussion of "disinvested" communities centers largely on the current condition of predominantly black neighborhoods, he does comment on the role of crime in immigrant communities historically. Specifically, Hagan contends that in an effort to make up for inequality accentuated by disinvestment, immigrant neighborhoods would reorganize to avail themselves of all available resources. Typically this reorganization meant that a disinvested community would "[adjust] to their situation by performing less desirable and sometimes illegitimate services for the majority group" (c.f. Hagan 1994, p. 78). Just as activities such as vice industries tended to concentrate in immigrant neighborhoods around the turn of the last century, Hagan (1994: 79) argues that a similar process of "disinvestment and recapitalization are central aspects of crime in contemporary urban America." In making this argument, Hagan preserves the fundamental argument of the social disorganization perspective (i.e., that the origins of crime are rooted in community social structure), while at the same time moving away from its ecological assumptive base.

A more common argument among the recent interpretations of the social disorganization perspective is that the relationship between community and crime is more sophisticated than that originally characterized by Shaw and McKay. For example, Heitgard and Bursik (1987) contend that a shortcoming of the social disorganization perspective is that it relies on a rigid, and somewhat arbitrary, definition of community. As Heitgard and Bursik (1987: 776) argue, the "overriding emphasis on the internal dynamics" of single geographical units is problematic because neighborhood processes often extend beyond administratively defined boundaries. More recent approaches relax this assumption and argue that neighborhood crime rates are influenced by both internal and external dynamics, thus viewing communities as part of a more integrated whole. Therefore, this broader view adheres to the notion that structural changes influence crime, however it dispenses with the assumption of the geographic independence of communities.

Another criticism of the classical social disorganization perspective is that it assumes a non-recursive causal relationship between crime and community characteristics (Liska and Bellair 1995; Liska, Logan, and Bellair 1998; Morenoff and Sampson 1997). Stated in causal terms, social disorganization theory posits that the observed level of crime in an area is influenced by a community's ecological structure. Social disorganization theorists base their explanations of crime on a single causal presupposition, never exploring the possibility that this causal logic may be incomplete. However, current scholarship acknowledges that while social structure certainly has an impact on crime, they argue that it is also important to recognize the influence of crime rates on the demographic profile of an area. By introducing the notion of reciprocal causation, contemporary researchers are able to account for a degree of neighborhood complexity that classical disorganization theory could not.

The critiques of the theory mentioned above raise important questions regarding how the theory was originally formulated. Despite these criticisms, however, it is worth pointing out the commonalities between the original and the more recent interpretations of social disorganization theory. Generally, the contemporary scholars accept the fundamental arguments advanced by the Chicago School theorists. That is, because the origins of crime are rooted in social structure, explanations of crime must consider the macro-level attributes of communities. The revisions are largely critiques of the overly simplified conceptualization of urban processes presented by Shaw and McKay. Further, it should be kept in mind that while the reinterpretations address legitimate shortcomings in the original theory, the criticisms are meant to refine, and ultimately to retain the theoretical tradition from which they derive.

A more recent trend in the social disorganization research literature is an emphasis on quantifying the influence of "intervening" community mechanisms on levels of crime. Instead of focusing exclusively on structure, this line of scholarship includes measures of characteristics "hypothesized to mediate the relationship between community structure and crime" (Sampson and Groves 1989, p. 775). A primary objective of this research is to explicate more clearly the causal process through which the structural composition of communities undermines their social control capacities. The work of Sampson and colleagues represents the most noteworthy attempt to refine empirical tests of the social disorganization perspective (Sampson and Groves 1989; Sampson and Raudenbush 1999; Sampson et al. 1997; Sampson et al. 2002). By mediating factors, Sampson and colleagues identify a number of characteristics (i.e., such as community cohesion, friendship networks, and involvement in local institutions) that are thought to be more directly related to levels of social control. Furthermore, Sampson argues that although the intervening processes are discussed in the original formulation of the theory, they have not been included in traditional tests of the theory.

Sampson and Groves (1989) offer the first test of whether intervening processes mediate the impact of social structure on crime, as disorganization theory suggests. Their study analyzes British Crime Survey (BCS) data, which contains self-reported criminal involvement information for a sample of British and Welsh individuals. Again, what is unique about the BCS data is that it includes information that can be used to gauge actual levels of social organization in communities. Rather than predicting crime using only the social structural characteristics of neighborhoods, Sampson and Groves (1989) include measures of three factors thought to mediate the impact of structural deprivation on crime; friendship networks, participation in local organizations, and unsupervised peer group activities. Again, the authors claim that with the inclusion of these endogenous factors, this study represents the first empirical test of the theory that is faithful to its causal explanations.

The results of their multivariate analyses find partial support for the hypotheses proposed by the social disorganization perspective. Sampson and Groves (1989) report that community structural characteristics are related to each of the three dimensions of social disorganization, as residential stability and ethnic heterogeneity are significant predictors of organizational participation and friendship networks. According to their findings, community structural characteristics have the strongest impact on unsupervised peer group activities. Moreover, Sampson and Groves (1989) find the measures of disorganization, and not the broader structural factors, to be the strongest predictors of both criminal involvement and victimization.

Although controlling for the "intervening" control mechanisms does not completely attenuate the direct effects structure, the authors conclude that their results provide strong support for the "power and generalizability" of the social disorganization perspective (Sampson and Groves 1989, p. 799).

Using survey data collected for Chicago neighborhoods, Sampson et al. (1997) also find evidence in support of the mediating effects hypothesis. In this study, Sampson et al. (1997) argue that a neighborhood's level of "collective efficacy" is likely to be a strong predictor of perceptions of crime, as well as actual levels of victimization and homicide. According to the authors, collective efficacy is a two-dimensional construct, one that includes elements of both social cohesion and social control. Sampson et at. (1997: 919) argue that it is the combination "of mutual trust and the willingness to intervene for the common good" that is indicative of a high degree of collective efficacy. Further, Sampson et al. (1997) propose that efficacy will mediate much of the effect of community structural disadvantage on neighborhood crime.

As a first test of their general hypothesis, the authors test the extent to which levels of collective efficacy are influenced by the broader neighborhood structural context. Consistent with the theoretical arguments, Sampson et al. (1997) find that social structural characteristics are significant predictors of collective efficacy. Specifically, the authors report that residential stability, immigrant concentration, and concentrated disadvantage are associated with neighborhood levels of social cohesion and social control. This research also finds that individuals living in areas characterized by higher levels of collective efficacy fear crime less than individuals living in structurally comparable areas with comparatively lower levels of efficacy. Similarly, areas characterized by a higher degree of collective efficacy have significantly lower levels of homicide and criminal victimization. Sampson et al. (1997: 922) interpret the finding that collective efficacy "partially mediates [the] widely cited relations between neighborhood social composition and violence" as further support for the tenets of social disorganization theory.

In a study that employs a unique data collection strategy called Systematic Social Observation (SSO), Sampson and Raudenbush (1999) conduct another empirical test for intervening social processes. To address this issue, the authors analyze a combination of census data, survey responses and observational data. The latter data source, which focuses mainly on visual evidence of community disorder, is constructed from observer logs and videotapes of neighborhoods around the city of Chicago.[7] Sampson and Raudenbush (1999) argue that the use of observational data makes an important contribution because such data provide information about levels of disorder that cannot be reliably captured using survey questionnaires alone. The measure of efficacy Sampson and Raudenbush (1999) use in this study is identical to the indicator included in the analysis discussed above.

According to Sampson and Raudenbush (1999: 636), the results from the multivariate analyses indicate a clear pattern in the data. First, the authors find that neighborhood structural factors are significantly related to observed levels of social and physical disorder. Specifically, economic deprivation and immigrant concentration are the strongest predictors of both physical and social disorder. Further, Sampson and Raudenbush (1999) confirm that residents also have accurate beliefs about levels of disorder in their communities. The results of the neighborhood survey, which asks individuals about disruption in their neighborhoods, correlate strongly with the observed levels of disorder. This finding indicates a degree of continuity between the perceptions of disorder held by an area's residents and observable neighborhood conditions. The main substantive finding of this research is that collective efficacy is associated with lower levels of violence, net of levels of physical and social disorder and other neighborhood structural characteristics. The authors conclude that these results are supportive of the expectations of social disorganization theory.

Additional research offers further evidence for the intervening effects of community-level social processes on levels of violence.[8] For example, in an analysis of Chicago neighborhoods that controls for both collective efficacy and local institutional involvement, Morenoff et al. (2001) find that collective efficacy predicts lower levels of violent offending and victimization. Further, Morenoff et al. (2001) find that collective efficacy partially attenuates structural influences on violence. The results of their analyses indicate that institutional involvement, such as membership in local voluntary organizations, is unrelated to levels of violent crime. In a related study, Warner and Roundtree

---

7   Sampson and Raudenbush (1999: 617-618) differentiate between two types of disorder; physical and social. Physical disorder refers to the presence of items such as cigarette butts, litter/garbage, gang graffiti, and drug paraphernalia. Social disorder refers to items such as loitering, public alcohol consumption, prostitutes, drug sales, and fighting.

8   For a more comprehensive review of criminological research on "neighborhood effects," see Sampson et al. (2002).

(1997) find that neighborhood cohesion, when measured as patterns of interpersonal interaction, is associated with lower levels of crime. Specifically, Warner and Roundtree (1997) report that the extent to which individuals engage in neighboring activities, is negatively associated with levels of assault. Interestingly, there is some evidence suggesting that this pattern is consistent across nations. In particular, in his analysis of a sample of cross-national neighborhood data, Lee (2000: 700) finds that community cohesion is also an "important determinant of victimization risk."

The findings from the "intervening processes" literature improve our understanding of the interplay between structural characteristics and social processes. Specifically, as the theory predicts, this body of research illustrates that local processes do have a mediating effect on the relationship between social structure and crime. Although the importance of controlling for intervening processes is recognized, such causal mechanisms will remain as unmeasured constructs in the analyses presented in this study. The primary reason is because available data sources do not allow for the inclusion of measures of collective efficacy or social cohesion. Data availability issues notwithstanding, the empirical results from the studies discussed above indicate that focusing on the direct effects of social structure on crime still contributes to our knowledge regarding neighborhood causal processes. This is evidenced by the fact that structural factors, such as poverty and residential stability, still emerge as significant predictors of violence, even after controlling for the presence of intervening mechanisms.

Conclusion

The social disorganization theory emerged during a period when American society was experiencing an unprecedented influx of immigrants. The social disorganization perspective, as does the urban ecological tradition more generally, pays particular attention to the impact that immigrants have on the social structure of the neighborhoods into which they settled. Largely, proponents of this theory argue that immigration has negative consequences for the urban communities receiving the newcomers. Because foreigners typically arrive in this country poor and lacking the human capital necessary for conventional success, the theory holds that they contribute both to levels of social disruption and the "relatively constant" levels of crime in the neighborhoods into which they settle (Shaw and McKay 1969 [1942], p. 315).

The issue of immigration has played a less central role in research designed to test social disorganization theory over time, with researchers focusing primarily on the social disorder of black neighborhoods. In part this is due to the fact that blacks are over-represented in arrest and victimization statistics and in part because often the disadvantages associated with urban poverty are borne disproportionately by blacks (Massey and Denton 1993; Wilson 1987, 1996). There is little disputing that black neighborhoods are "utterly unique" in the high and sustained levels of disadvantage experienced by their residents (Massey and Denton 1993, p. 2). However, according to the logic of the disorganization perspective, the theory would also expect immigration to have a positive effect on levels of crime. Nor do the contemporary reinterpretations of the theory offer arguments for why immigration should not be positively related to crime.

Following these arguments, social disorganization theory suggests a positive relationship between immigration and violent crime. Existing immigration/crime research focuses on the question of "is immigration related to crime?" Unlike the prior examinations of the disorganization perspective, this study poses a slightly different question, that being "how is immigration linked to observed levels of violence?" In other words, this research is sensitive to the possibility that immigration may influence crime through multiple causal channels. It is possible that immigration has a positive, yet indirect, effect on crime through its impact on an area's social structural characteristics. Similarly, it may also be true that immigration has a direct negative effect on violence. Considering both causal processes offers a broader view of the manner in which immigration and violent crime are related.

CHAPTER 3

Studies of Immigration and Crime:
Findings and Limitations of Previous Research

The study of the relationship between immigration and crime is not one that can be simply understood as "will increased immigration lead to an increase in amount of crimes committed in a given area?" The short answer is yes, we know that as the population expands, so does the volume of crimes committed due to the increase in the number of potential offenders (Hagan and Palloni 1998). The issue that criminologists focus on is whether immigration is associated with higher than expected increases in levels of criminal deviance. Crime researchers have addressed this question using one of two general approaches. The first is through individual-level analyses that examine immigrant involvement in crime. Such studies provide insight into the question of whether *immigrants* are involved disproportionately in the commission of criminal acts.

The second approach is less interested in the criminal behavior of individuals, focusing instead on the impacts of immigration, measured at the macro-level, on observed levels of crime. Using data measured at higher levels of aggregation (i.e., neighborhoods, cities, metropolitan areas), this line of scholarship is concerned with the extent to which the presence of an area's foreign-born population affects levels of crime, net of the structural and socio-demographic characteristics of an area. Studies falling into this category address the question of whether *immigration* is related to increased levels of crime.

The goal of this chapter is twofold; first, I will review the historical immigration/crime research dating back nearly a century, and second, I will discuss the findings reported in both the contemporary micro- and macro-level criminological research on this topic. Special attention is paid to the macro-level research because this study is designed as a test of social disorganization theory. The latter section also outlines some of the limitations associated with existing criminological research on immigration.

Historical Studies of Immigration and Crime

The earliest quantitative studies that focused explicitly on the immigrant/crime link began to emerge as rates of immigration peaked in the early decades of the twentieth century. Three separate reports issued during this period represent some of the earliest studies to take seriously the notion that there may be nativity differences in patterns of criminal offending. A 1901 report issued by the Industrial Commission concluded that foreign-born whites were less involved in crime than their native-born counterparts. This conclusion was supported in a report released by the Immigrant Commission a decade later. In 1911 the Immigrant Commission argued that there was no evidence indicating that immigrants contributed disproportionately to increases in crime.[9] The most extensive of the three reports, the "Wickersham Report," was released in 1931 by the National Commission on Law Observance and Enforcement. The conclusions drawn by the Wickersham Report are similar to those mentioned above that, in general, there was little evidence supporting the notion that foreigners engaged in higher levels of criminal activity than natives.

Exceptions to this general trend were also noted in the early immigration/crime research. For example, each of the reports mentioned disparities in levels of offending across immigrant generations. Increased involvement in criminal behavior was seen as a consequence of assimilating into American society, particularly for members of the second generation. The Wickersham Report also suggested that immigrants may be more likely to be involved in particular types of crime (i.e., homicide). The conclusions drawn in the early immigration/crime studies have been viewed with suspicion mainly because they were not based on careful empirical analyses. An author of one of the sections of the Wickersham report questioned the results from any criminological research conducted during this period because of the limitations of the data and the lack of methodological sophistication used to analyze them (see LaFree et al. 2000). Despite their methodological shortcomings, the early research was important because it recognized that immigration might have more than a simple, positive impact on crime. Interestingly, some of the questions raised in the earliest studies are the very same as those being addressed by contemporary researchers.

---

9   In this report the Commission indicated that Immigration may suppress crime rates (see Tonry 1997).

Contemporary Immigration Research

Immigrant Involvement in Crime

There is little disputing that immigrants, on average, arrive in the United States lacking many of the skills and resources necessary for conventional success (see Rumbaut et al. 2006). This pattern is not universal, as members of some immigrant groups arrive in the United States with valuable occupational or educational training (see Massey 1995; Alba et al. 1999). Nevertheless, the fact remains that upon arrival, many immigrants lack the human capital (e.g., job training, English proficiency, formal education), which would help to smooth their transition into life in American society. Butcher and Piehl (1998a) point out that this lack of marketable skills may lead to a higher level of criminal engagement among immigrants. The authors speculate that when confronted with "poorer legal sector opportunities" illegitimate opportunities may become increasingly attractive for foreigners (Butcher and Piehl 1998a, p. 655).

Moreover, immigrants have limited residential options and tend to settle in more disadvantaged neighborhoods. The 2000 Census reports that the average immigrant lives in an area that is poorer, is comprised of fewer college graduates, and has a higher unemployment rate than the average neighborhood of a native-born individual.[10] The differences are even more pronounced when the characteristics of the neighborhoods inhabited by recent immigrants are compared to those of natives. Following this logic, the immigrant involvement hypothesizes proposes that he combination of narrow occupational and residential opportunities gives reason to believe that immigrants will have an increased likelihood of criminal involvement. Due to the hardship endured by immigrants, it stands to reason that the "ethnicity of criminals and their victims [will reflect] the recency of arrival in this country" (Short 1997, p. 7).

Implicit in the immigrant involvement hypothesis is the notion that the likelihood of engaging in criminal behavior diminishes as a product of time spent in the United States. In other words, this perspective proposes that as immigrants assimilate, their involvement in crime will decrease. Yet there is also empirical evidence to suggest that assimilation into American society, measured as either time spent in the

---

10 US Census 2000 SF3 data for individuals living in metropolitan areas (http://mumford.albany.edu/census/SepUneq/PublicSeparateUnequal.htm).

United States or immigrant generation, is associated with an increased likelihood of criminal involvement or other forms of deviant conduct. For example, research has shown that immigrants are less likely to receive public assistance, have lower levels of non-marital fertility, and have higher levels of academic achievement than their native-born individuals (Zhou and Bankston 1998, 2006; Kao and Tienda 1995; Tienda and Jenson 1988). Although none of these factors is a direct measure of criminal involvement, these results do suggest a general pro-social orientation among immigrants, a pattern that has been characterized as the "immigration paradox" (see Rumbaut 1997; see also Sampson and Bean 2006).

A similar point is made by Zhou and Bankston (1998) who report that second (and later) generation Vietnamese adolescents are significantly more likely to engage in delinquent activities than foreign-born youths. Furthermore, the authors provide evidence that the delinquents have more characteristics in common with US born individuals than with the first generation Vietnamese. In a recent follow-up study, Zhou and Bankston (2006) conclude that this pattern has remained stable over the past decade. This suggests that, as many community members contend, the "over-Americanization" of these youths is at the root of their deviant behavior. The limited scope of the Zhou and Bankston studies make it difficult to generalize their findings to the wider population. However, results raise questions regarding the straight-line assimilation model advanced by social disorganization theory.

Moving beyond the analysis of a single ethnic community, research also fails to provide clear support for assertion that assimilation into American society reduces the likelihood of criminal participation. For example, in a study of self-reported criminal behavior and convictions for a sample of adolescents and young adults (ages 15-23), Butcher and Piehl (1998b: 483) find that younger, unemployed males are the most likely to report engaging in criminal acts; findings that mirror results presented in much criminological research. However, the authors report that immigrants are significantly less likely than their native-born counterparts to report committing a crime, being convicted, or coming into contact with a criminal justice agency (i.e., police, courts). Butcher and Piehl (1998b) interpret these results as evidence that immigrants—and particularly younger immigrants—do not engage in crime at levels significantly higher than natives.

Researchers have also used rates of institutionalization to gauge levels of immigrant involvement in crime. The focus on institutionalization is justified due to the fact that some scholars argue that immigrants are over-represented in American correctional institutions (McDonald 1997; Scalia 1996). However, Hagan and Palloni (1999) argue that a partial explanation for the elevated rates for immigrants is due to pre-incarceration factors, rather than immigrant criminality. Specifically, Hagan and Palloni (1999) report that part of the reason for immigrant over-representation in prisons is attributable to the elevated chances of pre-trial detention for foreigners. Once imprisonment rates are adjusted to account for their increased likelihood pre-trial incapacitation, Hagan and Palloni (1999: 626) show that immigrants in El Paso and San Diego are incarcerated at lower rates than natives.

In a national study of institutionalization rates among recent and non-recent immigrants from 1970-1990, Butcher and Piehl (1998a) report that immigrants are institutionalized at lower levels than individuals born in the US. Additionally, the authors find that recent immigrants, measured as those who arrived within the past five years, are committed to institutions at lower levels than non-recent immigrants. The lower level of institutionalization experienced by recent immigrants emerges, despite the fact that they have the lowest levels of human capital (measured as educational attainment). Although the authors are unable to identify the specific institutional settings of respondents, Butcher and Piehl (1998a: 677) conclude that "if natives had the same institutionalization probabilities as immigrants, our jails and prisons would have one-third fewer inmates."[11]

The weight of the research reviewed above indicates that immigrants are not involved in crime at disproportionately higher levels than their native-born counterparts. Despite initial deficits in human capital, the research on immigrant involvement in crime consistently shows that immigrants generally engage in criminal activity at lower levels than native-born individuals. Such findings are at odds with expectations of the disorganization perspective, which holds that the social conditions experienced by many immigrants will promote criminal behavior. Although the research suggests that immigrants

---

11 The Census Public Use Microdata Sample (PUMS) data used in this study includes a variety of institutional settings in the measure of institutionalization (e.g., prisons, mental hospitals, drug treatment centers, retirement homes). However, in order to capture mainly the prison population, this analysis includes only males aged 18-40.

themselves may be less likely to engage in crime, these findings do not speak to the broader question of how immigration influences levels of crime in the areas into which the foreign-born settle. Research focusing on this topic is reviewed in the following section.

The Effects of Immigration on Crime

The amount of criminological research conducted on immigration varies proportionally with overall rates of immigration. When levels of immigration ebbed during the middle of the last century, relatively little academic attention was paid to this topic. Similarly, as rates of immigration increased over the past decade, criminologists have shown a renewed interest in understanding the extent to which patterns of criminal behavior are tied to the influx of foreigners (see Martinez 2002). Although immigration research has the potential to inform many crime theories, much of the recent research tests hypotheses derived from the social disorganization perspective. Below is a review of the findings in the contemporary research literature.

A current trend among criminological research is to focus on variations in crime rates across relatively small geographical areas (i.e., neighborhoods) (Miethe and McDowell 1993; Roundtree et al. 1994; Morenoff and Sampson 1997).[12] Following in this tradition, neighborhood-level data are commonly used by many of the contemporary crime scholars who study immigration. This is particularly true of the work of Martinez who, along with colleagues, has undertaken the most extensive research program on the connection between immigration and crime (Martinez 2002; Martinez and Lee 2000a; Lee et al. 2001; Lee 2003; Lee and Martinez 2002; Nielsen et al. 2005). The research conducted by Martinez is highly specialized, as it focuses largely on the influence of immigration on homicide victimization within Hispanic neighborhoods.[13] Despite the refined scope of this body of literature, the findings reported by Martinez and colleagues have implications for the current study because they provide the most systematic tests of the immigrant/crime link to date.

---

12 The definition of a neighborhood tends to correspond to census definitions such as blocks, block groups, or tracts.

13 Martinez recognizes that the term Hispanic includes both native and foreign-born individuals. However, because the cities under investigation attract large numbers of immigrants, the Hispanic populations are disproportionately comprised of immigrants.

In *Latino Homicide* (2002) Martinez compares neighborhood structural conditions and homicide rates between Hispanic and non-Hispanic racial groups in five American cities (Miami, El Paso, San Diego, Chicago, and Houston). Using racially and ethnically disaggregated victimization data, Martinez (2002) finds that rates of Hispanic homicide victimization are consistently higher than similar rates for non-Hispanic whites and lower than those for non-Hispanic blacks. The methodology employed in this analysis is largely descriptive, but Martinez points out that Hispanics are victims of homicides at lower rates than non-Hispanic blacks, despite the fact that both groups live in structurally similar neighborhoods. Indeed, Martinez (2002: 141) argues that rates of Latino homicide are lower than expected given the levels structural disadvantage of many Hispanic neighborhoods. In *Latino Homicide,* Martinez never uses multivariate techniques as a means of empirically documenting the negative effect of immigration on rates of killing, although this is the logical implication of his findings.

There is quantitative evidence in the research literature of a negative direct effect of immigration on violent crime. Again using racially disaggregated homicide data for three cities, Lee et al. (2001; see also Lee 2003) find that the size of the recently arrived immigrant population in Miami is inversely related to levels of homicide. For the other two cities under investigation (El Paso and San Diego), the authors report that immigration has insignificant effects on lethal violence in all but one of the regression analyses. The authors interpret the combination of negative and null findings as non-supportive of either theoretical expectations or popular sentiment regarding the association between immigration and crime (Lee et al. 2001, p. 571). Similarly, in a study of Chicago neighborhoods that collected observational data using the systematic social observation method, Sampson and Raudenbush (1999) report an inverse association between community levels of "concentrated immigration" and robbery rates.[14] The research mentioned above does offer some support for disorganization theory in that social structural factors such as poverty and residential instability have significant positive effects on violence.

While research has shown that immigration is not associated with higher levels of crime across neighborhoods, other studies examine this

---

14   The "concentrated immigration" variable is an index comprised of % Latino, % foreign-born, and the density of children (% of persons aged 6-15).

relationship using larger areal units. In their study of the impacts of non-citizen and illegal immigration on 1980 metropolitan arrest rates, Hagan and Palloni (1998) find that the size of the illegal immigrant population is unrelated to either violent or property arrest rates (see also US Commission on Immigration Reform 1994). Although Hagan and Palloni (1998: 380) report that the number of non-citizens is related to an increase in property arrests, they conclude that "there is no compelling or systematic evidence at the SMSA level that immigration causes crime." Similarly, in a study of 43 metropolitan areas, Butcher and Piehl (1998b) find that while immigrants generally tend to settle in areas with high crime rates, changes in the size of the immigrant population between 1980 and 1990 are unrelated to changes in either overall or violent crime rates.

A series of studies also shows that Latino-specific homicide rates are influenced by the structural conditions of cities. In a study comparing victimization rates in Miami and El Paso, Lee et al. (2000) find that killings involving Hispanics are distributed similarly across homicide types (i.e., acquaintance, intimate, stranger) in both cities. The authors conclude that the higher number of homicides committed in Miami is reflective of the more violent urban and regional contexts in that area of the country. Similarly, using a sample of 111 US cities, Martinez (1996) finds that economic inequality between Hispanics is associated with increased levels of Hispanic homicide victimization. A similar finding is reported by Martinez (2000) who reports that immigration is associated with increased levels of felony homicides (i.e., those committed during the commission of another crime). Martinez (2000) concludes that the increase in felony homicides in areas with large Hispanic immigrant populations is likely the result of increased contact with other non-Hispanics (see also Blau 1977). It is important to note a more general trend in these studies; namely, that the social structural characteristics emerge as significant predictors of homicide, a pattern that is consistent with the expectations of social disorganization theory.

Two general conclusions can be drawn from the existing research on immigration on crime. First, the weight of the evidence suggests that immigration is not associated with increased levels of crime. To the extent that a relationship does exist, the literature consistently finds a negative effect of immigration on levels of crime, and particularly lethal violence. This finding stands in contrast to the theoretical logic of the social disorganization perspective. Second, the criminological research on immigration also finds partial support for disorganization theory, evidenced by the strong and significant impacts of social structural characteristics on levels of crime. Just as disorganization perspective proposes, indicators such as poverty and residential instability are found to be positively related to crime. In light of these contrasting results, immigration researchers generally interpret the unexpected negative impact of immigration on crime as a limitation of social disorganization theory.

Limitations of Immigration/Crime Research

The mixed support for the social disorganization perspective offered by the existing research on this topic raises questions as to whether the theory accurately describes the impact of immigration on crime. The findings discussed above do suggest that the theory mischaracterizes the nature of this relationship. Nevertheless, it is important to recognize that the extant research does not address a number of questions that may have implications for this conclusion. For example, contemporary research does not directly test the assimilationist logic informing the ecological perspective. A central argument of social disorganization theory is that over time immigrant populations are incorporated into the American social system. Therefore, the theory posits that, as length of time in the U.S. increases, immigrant groups will achieve higher social standing, and will be less likely live in structurally disadvantaged (high crime) areas. This position is more clearly illustrated in the work of Lane (1989) who attributes the decline in Italian homicide rates during the early decades of the last century, to their increased incorporation into the conventional labor market.

Implicit in this assertion is the notion that immigration does not have a universal impact on crime. Rather, the theory proposes that the immigrant/crime link is likely to be less pronounced in areas where much of the foreign-born population has had time to assimilate into American society. Conversely, the social disorganization perspective holds that the association between immigration and crime will be the strongest in communities with the largest presence of the recent immigrants. Previous research offers little support for this theoretical assertion, however. Still research has generally failed to take into consideration the full complement of differences among the foreign-born population when examining the impact of immigration on crime. Instead of testing for differential impacts across multiple dimensions of immigrant status, researchers have continued to focus on recency of arrival. I argue that by assuming the impact on crime to be consistent across the immigrant population, prior research has neglected to test an important theoretical precept.

Although the logic of the disorganization perspective concedes that certain characteristics of the immigrant population (i.e., time in the US) may have differential impacts on neighborhood violence, this topic was not fully developed in the original theoretical formulation. One difference that was not discussed by theorists was the national origin, or ethnicity, of newcomers. The theory does not address the degree to which structural conditions vary as a product of the presence of a given ethnic immigrant group. In addition, current research has also neglected to examine the potential causal differences between specific immigrant ethnicities and crime.[15] A notable exception is the work of Martinez and Lee (1998) who show that in Miami, Cuban and Haitian immigrants were less involved in violence relative to group size than the non-Hispanic whites (see also Martinez and Lee 2000b; Reid et al. 2005; Lee and Martinez 2006). However, this study does not directly address the question of the degree to which levels of crime are influenced by the presence of either of these groups. A comparison of the effects of immigration on crime between ethnic groups is warranted, particularly given the diversity of the contemporary immigrant stream (Kleniewski 1997; Massey 1995; Alba et al. 1999). In this study, I examine the question of differential causality by comparing the effects on crime for the largest immigrant ethnic groups in each of the cities under investigation.

There is another closely related issue that merits further discussion here; that is, the notion of immigrant generation. The concept of immigrant generation classifies members of an immigrant population according to their nativity and ethnic origins. Specifically, members of a given ethnic group are identified as falling into one of three generational categories. The first generation is comprised exclusively of foreign-born individuals. Members of the second generation are individuals who are born in the United States to foreign-born parents. That is, the second generation is made up of the children of immigrants. The third generation is composed of individuals born in the United States to native-born parents. The definition of generation allows researchers to locate and compare social outcomes for those with recent ties to immigration. Furthermore, research has illustrated that these

---

15 The majority of the work of Martinez and colleagues examines the effects of broadly defined Hispanic immigration on homicide, but this research does not test for differences within this general categorization (Martinez and Lee 2002; Martinez 2000; see also Lee 2003).

generational distinctions capture substantively important differences between co-ethnics and contribute to a more complete understanding of immigrant experiences in American society.

In their discussion of immigrant intergenerational assimilation patterns, Portes and Zhou (1993, 1994) argue that members of the first generation, despite their low pay and difficult working conditions, are likely to apply pro-social solutions to their disadvantaged social positions (see also Kao 1995). This is consistent with the previously mentioned "optimism" hypothesis, which suggests that foreign-born individuals evaluate their current situations as comparatively better than they were in their countries of origin. However, research also suggests that the second generation may be less likely to share this positive outlook regarding their prospects for social mobility (Portes and Zhou 1993; Portes and Rumbaut 2001). Lacking experience in a foreign society as a comparative model, those belonging to the second generation are likely to evaluate their opportunities according to American societal expectations. Based on the differences in perspective across a generation, the children of immigrants may believe that their chances for conventional success are limited.

The perception held by the children of immigrants that they will experience limited opportunities for upward mobility may have implications for their levels of criminal involvement. Portes and Zhou (1993: 89) contend there is an increasing likelihood that members of the second generation will become involved in "reactive subculture[s] as a means of protecting their senses of self worth." Often, these subcultures adopt "oppositional ideologies" and their members are less likely to be involved social institutions such as school or conventional employment (Portes and Rumbaut 2001, p. 60). The decreased levels of institutional involvement are likely to be associated with an increased likelihood of engaging in criminal activities (see Perlmann and Waldinger (1997) for alternative explanations).

While never studied directly, the possibility of generational disparities in criminal offending was mentioned in the Wickersham Report (1931), one of the earliest studies of the immigrant/crime link. Similarly, the more recent research by Zhou and Bankston (1998, 2006) provides some empirical support for the notion that native-born ethnics may have an increased likelihood of criminal involvement. However, examining the extent to which criminal behavior varies as a product of immigrant generation is a topic that has been neglected by criminologists. The lack of attention to this important aspect of the immigration experience, on either micro- or macro-levels, illustrates that the study of immigration and crime would benefit from the use of more precise measures of immigration, similar to those employed in the non-criminological immigration research literature (for exceptions see Morenoff and Astor 2006; Sampson and Bean 2006).

Although I recognize this as an important limitation of immigrant/crime research in general, the subject of intergenerational differences is not addressed in this study. Due to the limitations of available data, I will not be able to examine generation as a dimension of immigration as it relates to levels of criminal violence.[16] While academic interest in the immigrant/crime link is growing, there remain a number of important research areas, which have yet to be fully explored.

There is also a methodological issue surrounding the prior criminological studies of immigration and their subsequent conclusions that deserves further attention. One limitation of the contemporary immigration/crime studies is that they do not test whether immigration is a destabilizing social force. That is, none of the research examines the impact of immigration on the structural composition of an area. The notion that immigration contributes to observed levels of disorder is an important aspect of social disorganization theory. Without information about this fundamental relationship, the extant research findings should be interpreted with some caution.

Measuring this relationship requires modeling a causal structure that is more consistent with the one hypothesized by classical disorganization theory. In addition to being more parsimonious theoretically, controlling for the indirect effects of immigration on structural factors is important because doing so may influence substantive findings. It is not clear how the modified causal model will influence the observed direct effect of immigration on crime. There is the possibility that immigration will have the strongest impact on social structure, and once the indirect effects are specified, the strong negative influence on crime will be attenuated, or reduced to non-significance. Such a finding would be seen as supportive of the disorganization perspective. Similarly, it may be that the influence of immigration on crime operates through both direct and indirect causal mechanisms. Pointing out possible alternative relationships between immigration and

---

16 Census 2000 provides data tables iterated for specific ethnic groups. From some of the tables it is possible to identify the number of foreign-born ethnic group members. However, from these data it is not possible to distinguish between members of the second and third (or higher) generations (see Portes and Rumbaut 2001, p. 33).

crime is not to say that the conclusions drawn in contemporary research are necessarily incorrect, but rather that they provide an incomplete picture of a complicated causal process.

Despite the increasing use of sophisticated statistical/analytical techniques, I argue that by not testing for the "disorganizing" effects of immigration, it is difficult for researchers to evaluate fully social disorganization theory (see Martinez 2002; Lee et al. 2000; Lee 2003; Lee and Martinez 2002). By considering how immigration impacts both crime and the social structural characteristics of an area, this study addresses a shortcoming of contemporary immigration research. Further, the broader view taken in this study will cast new light on a relationship that scholars have been debating for nearly a century.

Research Hypotheses

Immigration and Social Structure

Theoretical insights in combination with the empirical findings discussed above allow for the development of a set of hypotheses to be tested in this research. The leading hypothesis in this study is that immigration is associated with increased levels of social disorder. A key argument made by social disorganization theory is that immigrants tend to be channeled into disadvantaged areas because they possess lower levels of human capital. Further, the deficits in human capital relegate many immigrants to low-paying occupations, which contributes to the overall poverty rates. For these reasons, I hypothesize that immigration will be positively related to an area's level of economic deprivation.

Similarly, social disorganization theory argues that disadvantaged neighborhoods experience high rates of population turnover, with residents leaving once they acquire the skills and experience necessary to achieve a higher social standing. However, the assimilationist logic informing this perspective presents an oversimplified picture of the outmigration process. Some immigrants are likely to treat the initial neighborhoods into which they settle as temporary "way stations." Still, this straight-line assimilation model will not apply to the many immigrants who become "ensnared" in disadvantaged neighborhoods and are unable to move out (Logan et al. 2002, p. 301). Nor can this explanation account for residential preference, meaning that some will choose not to move, despite opportunities to do so. Due to the complexities of the outmigration process, I hypothesize that immigration, broadly defined, will not be associated with increased levels of residential instability. Because residential stability is a measure of time spent in a given location, it does seem that the size of the recent immigrant population, by definition, will be positively related to residential instability.

Although immigrants are arriving in the United States at rates that rival those of previous periods, the current wave is unique in its broad racial and ethnic composition (Kleniewski 1997; Massey 1995). Due to the increased diversity of the immigrant population, it follows that immigration will have a positive impact on the racial/ethnic diversity of an area. Because there are no clear reasons to expect recency of immigration to impact heterogeneity differentially, I hypothesize that immigration, measured either as all foreign-born or recent arrivals, will have a similar effect on heterogeneity.

Social Structure and Crime

The social disorganization theory argues that social structural factors will be related to increased levels of violent crime. Indeed, a large body of research literature has successfully documented this relationship. A comprehensive review of this body of literature would be largely an exercise in replication, as many of the findings are consistent across studies. The effects of structure on crime have not been universal, however, and do warrant some further discussion, paying attention to exceptional findings. Economic deprivation, measured in absolute or relative terms, is a strong predictor crime. The economic viability of an area has been shown to be a significant predictor of overall levels of violent and non-violent offending, as well as race-specific rates of crime (see Sampson and Lauritsen 1997; Sampson 1987; Shihadeh and Flynn 1996; Parker and McCall 1999; Warner and Pierce 1993). The immigration/crime literature also finds that neighborhood economic conditions influence crime; therefore, a positive relationship between poverty and violent crime is expected.

Ecological theory argues that population shifts contribute to disorder because the turnover makes it difficult for residents to establish strong relationships with other residents or attachments to place. Lacking such bonds, residents become less concerned about and less involved in neighborhood activities, creating a context in which mechanisms of social control are less effective. Residential instability is a factor that has been shown to be related to increased levels of crime (see Bursik and Grasmick 1993; Sampson and Groves 1989). The immigration research also finds support for the residential instability hypothesis (see Lee 2003; Lee et al. 2001).

Warner and Pierce (1993) find the opposite to be true; that is, that residential *stability* is related to increased levels of robbery and assault. The authors argue that this effect reflects the frustration associated with conditions of extreme social isolation and lack of opportunities experienced by many blacks living in "neighborhoods of last resort" (Warner and Pierce 1993, p. 507). Although they may be economically disadvantaged, it is less likely that the neighborhoods into which immigrants settle fit this "last resort" classification. Moreover, because prior immigration research finds residential instability to be positively related to violent crime, a similar effect is hypothesized here.

The social disorganization theory posits that areas with racially/ethnically mixed populations are likely to have correspondingly high rates of crime. The logic underpinning this position is that cultural and/or language differences in diverse communities make it difficult for residents to establish the strong social networks necessary to buffer against crime. Prior research has found support for this claim (see Warner and Pierce 1993; Sampson and Groves 1989). Overall measures of heterogeneity are uncommon in the immigration research literature, so I cannot base my expectations on prior immigration studies. However, drawing from theoretical expectations and prior findings, I hypothesize that heterogeneity will have a positive impact on violence.

Based on the preceding discussion, it is hypothesized that the impact of structural factors on the various indicators of crime will follow theoretical expectations. I submit that the structural characteristics of an area will have similar effects on crime, regardless of which measure of violence is included in the analytical models. It is not necessary to describe the different ways in which structure will impact various violent crimes. In part this is because there are no theoretical grounds for expecting the effects of structure on crime to differ. The theory speaks generally about the positive relationship between disorganization and crime, yet this perspective does not claim to be a better predictor of any particular type of criminal deviance. This position is also justified by the fact that the research has found consistent support for the theory predicting both violent and non-violent crimes.

To this point, the research hypotheses have focused on the indirect consequences of immigration on violent crime. This topic is not completely new to immigration research, although it has not been a primary focus. For example, Martinez (2002: 138) argues that "immigration did drive up the Latino poverty rate, but it also strengthened communities," which suggests that levels of violence are influenced by both direct and indirect causal processes. The extent to which immigration promotes structural disadvantage (e.g., poverty), will indicate a positive indirect effect on crime. Additionally, if immigration also increases the number of hard-working, motivated, and goal-oriented individuals in a neighborhood, this suggests that immigration may have a negative direct effect on crime.

The majority of criminological research on immigration focuses on the latter relationship; that is, measuring the direct impact of immigration on crime. The balance of the empirical evidence gives reason to suspect that immigration is associated with lower levels of violence. However, because research has concentrated primarily on homicide a question remains as to whether this pattern holds when more broadly defined indicators of violence are analyzed. Some scholars contend that although immigrants are less likely to commit homicides, they will be more likely to become involved in other less-serious types of crime (Hagan and Palloni 1999). This point is largely speculative, as research has yet to document this proposed relationship. Due to the consistency of the results in the crime literature, coupled with those in the immigrant optimism/selectivity research it is hypothesized here that immigration will not have a systematic positive impact on levels of criminal violence. While a negative (or null) direct relationship is expected, it is likely that the magnitude of this effect will vary across the different indicators of violence.

Conclusion

Quantitative research has analyzed the relationship between immigration and crime both at the micro- and macro-levels. The individual-level analyses focus on whether foreign-born individuals are involved in crime at disproportionately higher levels than natives. Results from the earliest historical studies have been somewhat mixed, showing that immigrants may have higher levels of involvement in some types of crime (i.e., homicide). More generally, the historical research on immigration finds little support for the notion that immigrants have a higher criminal propensity than natives. Contemporary research has examined immigrant representation in crime using both self-reported criminal involvement and data regarding institutional commitments of immigrants. Both types of research draw similar conclusions regarding the relationship between immigration and crime; that is, despite arriving in the United States with deficits in human capital, immigrants have lower levels of criminal engagement than their native-born counterparts.

A majority of the research on this topic examines the effects of immigration, measured in the aggregate, on crime. The preponderance of existing immigration research uses homicide as the indicator of criminal deviance. Using cities or neighborhoods as the units of analysis, these studies typically find mixed support for social disorganization theory. As the theory expects, structural conditions such as high rates of poverty and residential instability are associated with increased levels of crime. However, the size of the immigrant population is often found to have a direct negative effect on crime, a result that is interpreted as contrary to theoretical expectations. Although most current studies focus exclusively on lethal violence, research has found little support for the claim that that immigration is related to increases in overall or violent crime rates.

The hypotheses tested in the current study are derived from current immigration research. This study departs from conventional immigration research because it does not focus exclusively on the direct impact of immigration on violent crime. In addition to testing for the direct effects of immigration, this research also examines the extent to which immigration has a disorganizing effect the social structural characteristics of an area. This represents an improvement over prior research because it will yield a more complete view of the various causal channels through which immigration may influence levels of violence. Further, because this study examines the impact of immigration on a wider array of violent criminal outcomes, it offers a broader view of the connection between immigration and crime.

CHAPTER 4

Analytical Approach:
Data and Methodology Employed in Current Study

To review briefly, the purpose of the present study is to examine the association between immigration and violent crime. Recent research offers little empirical support for the purported immigrant/crime link. Indeed, research generally finds a negative relationship between the size of the foreign-born population and violence, and in particular homicide. Scholars interpret this negative relationship as a limitation in the explanatory power of social disorganization theory. Although the inverse association between immigration and crime is a consistent finding in the literature, it does not provide a complete view of the manner in which these two factors may be associated. There are a number of ways in which the current study improves upon existing immigration research. This research project represents an initial test for the "disorganizing" effects of immigration, because it considers both the direct and indirect effects of immigration on violent crime. In addition, this study also examines the immigrant/crime link using multiple indicators of violence, which casts light on the generalizability of the findings reported in the existing literature.

Data Sources

This research analyzes patterns of violent crime in three cities: Miami, Florida; Houston, Texas; and Alexandria, Virginia. Each of these cities is well-suited for inclusion in this study because the foreign-born comprise substantial portions of their total populations (see Table 4.1). For example, immigrants account for nearly sixty percent of the population for the city of Miami. Although the sizes of the foreign-born populations are proportionally smaller in Houston and Alexandria, still more than a quarter of the residents in each of these cities were born outside of the United States (26.4% and 25.4%, respectively). Additionally, the foreign-born populations in these cities reflect the

Immigration and Crime

Table 4.1. Largest Foreign-born Regional Immigrant Populations by City, 2000.

	Miami	%	Houston	%	Alexandria	%
Total Population	362,470		1,953,631		128,283	
Total Foreign Born	215,739	59.5	516,105	26.4	32,600	25.4
Europe	4,506	2.1	23,294	4.5	2,790	8.6
Asia	2,260	1.0	92,366	17.9	8,059	24.7
Africa	449	0.2	16,988	3.3	7,665	23.5
Americas	208,483	96.6	382,527	74.1	14,024	43.0
Caribbean	135,541	62.8	9,904	1.9	811	2.5
Central America	52,690	24.4	351,119	68.0	9,772	30.0
South America	19,739	9.1	17,256	3.3	2,974	9.1
North America	513	0.2	4,248	0.8	467	1.4

Source: Census 2000 Summary File 3.

increased diversity of the current wave of immigration (Kleniewski 1997; Butcher and Piehl 1998a; Massey 1995). This is particularly true in Houston, where nearly ninety percent of foreigners are either Hispanic (primarily from Mexico and Central America) or Asian, as compared to seventy percent in Alexandria. Similar to Houston, the immigrant population in Miami is disproportionately Hispanic (87.1%), yet it is unique in that the immigrants who settle in this city are largely of Afro-Caribbean origin.

In this study, tract-level data gathered from two administrative sources are analyzed. The measures of violent crime include offenses known to the police and were collected from official police department records. The data for Alexandria and Houston were collected under a project headed by Dr. Lauren Krivo and Dr. Ruth Peterson titled "Understanding Crime and Community: A National Neighborhood Crime Study." The data for these two cities include the number of violent offenses that occurred between 1999 and 2001. The data for Miami spans the same time period and was originally collected by Dr.

Ramiro Martinez. The Miami data contain information about the number of criminal offenses known to the police.

The analysis of neighborhood-level crime data is increasingly common in the criminological research literature (see Sampson et al. 1997; Morenoff and Sampson 1997; Miethe and McDowell 1993; Roundtree et al. 1994). Data collected for smaller geographic areas are attractive because they allow researchers to look more carefully at how criminal behavior is distributed across ecological areas. Such variations are masked in the summary measures of crime provided for larger areal units (i.e., cities, counties, states). Thus, the emergence of crime data gathered for neighborhoods has allowed scholars to examine how processes operate on smaller scales and within specific social contexts.

A potential limitation of the use of neighborhood-level data is that there may be locational disparities between the residence of offenders (or victims) and the commission of crimes. It is important to recognize that the areas in which crimes are committed do not always correspond to those in which the offenders (or victims) reside. However, research examining this "journey-to-crime" phenomenon indicates that most violent crimes are committed in very close proximity to where offenders live (Rossmo 2000; Lu 2003; Wiles and Costello 2000; McIver 1981). Researchers have also found that this pattern holds even among more active offenders. In a study of criminal patterns in Miami, Rhodes and Conly (1981) present evidence that the journey-to-crime operates as a distance-decay function, meaning that the number of crimes committed decreases as a function of distance away from where the offender resides (see also Paulsen and Robinson 2004).

Prior research also finds that on average, violent offenders travel the shortest distances to crime, relative to criminals who engage in other forms of deviant conduct (Rossmo 2000; Rhodes and Conly 1981). For example, studies have shown that homicides, rapes, and aggregated assaults are the crimes that tend to be committed nearest to offenders' homes (see Gabor and Gottheil 1984; Rossmo 2000, p. 105-110). Robberies tend to take place further distances from criminal residences, but the travel distances to robbery are still shorter than comparative trips for less serious property-based offenses. The majority of robberies are still committed less than a mile from where perpetrators live, suggesting that there is a high probability that such crimes will occur in the home neighborhoods of offenders (Reppetto 1976). Although there is bound to be some slippage in the data, prior research has clearly illustrated that "while criminals are mobile, they don't seem to go very far in committing a crime" (McIver 1981, p. 22). Information regarding the structural characteristics of neighborhoods is extracted from the 2000 Census Summary Files 1 (SF1) and 3 (SF3). The data available in SF1 contain information for a full enumeration of the U.S. population. Because SF1 provides detailed tables for race and ethnic groups iterated by age and Hispanic origin, these data are used to construct indicators of neighborhood demographic composition. SF3 data, which are derived from a representative sample of households, are used to construct the remaining variables to be used in this research. Included in the list of variables drawn from the SF3 release are the counts of the foreign-born populations, as well as levels of poverty, unemployment, and residential stability. The data preparation was done in two steps. The first involved drawing extractions from the Census files and constructing the variables to be included in the analytical models. The second required using a GIS application to geo-reference the crime incidents and to match them to the Census records.

Analytical Approach

Chapter 5 provides a detailed descriptive account of the cities included in this study is provided. The descriptive information offers an overview of the broader urban contexts that are the settings for this research. Specifically, the descriptive analyses present information about the social structural characteristics of the cities as a whole as well as for the typical immigrant neighborhoods. Information regarding the "typical" immigrant neighborhoods is computed using a series of exposure (P*) indices (see Logan 2002). The exposure indices highlight variations in social structural characteristics between immigrant ethnic neighborhoods within a given city. Moreover, the exposure indices allow for the comparison of the conditions in the average immigrant neighborhoods between cities.

Additionally, Chapter 5 includes a section devoted to descriptive spatial analysis. This section presents maps depicting the spatial distributions of the foreign-born population and each of the measures of violent crime to be used in this research. The maps are created using the latest Exploratory Spatial Data Analytic (ESDA) techniques (see Anselin et al. 2000; Griffiths and Chavez 2004). Specifically, I present univariate moran scatterplot maps, which provide graphical representations of statistical information regarding the presence of spatial autocorrelation (see Baller et al. 2001). The moran scatterplot technique is sensitive to departures from spatial randomness, and the corresponding maps show the extent to which similar values on a given indicator concentrate geographically. If areas with high levels of immigrants cluster geographically, this suggests that foreign-born individuals are channeled into similar areas in the city. The examination of the spatial distributions of violent crime is also a useful tool for assessing whether the outcome variables are spatially autocorrelated (Anselin et al. 2000). Together, the descriptive information provided in this chapter offers contextual information that cannot be observed in the multivariate analyses.

The results from the multivariate analyses, which test for the full range of effects of immigration on violence, are presented in Chapter 6. Unlike previous research, the present study examines both the direct and indirect effects of immigration on violence. The full range of effects of immigration is estimated using a two-step process. The initial regression results focus on the disorganization theory's claim that immigration is a disruptive, or socially disorganizing, process. As mentioned previously, the theory expects that immigration will have negative consequences for the social structural composition of the neighborhoods into which foreigners settle. To test this notion, Ordinary Least Squares (OLS) regression methods were used to estimate the impact of immigration on the structural factors associated with social disorganization. Regression models are also run for the largest immigrant ethnic groups in each city, in an effort to detect whether immigration has differential impacts on community social structure, and by extension levels of violent crime. Although tests for the "disorganizing" impact of immigration on neighborhood structure are consistent with theoretical explanations, they have not been included in prior immigration/crime research.

A second set of results, which focus on the effects of immigration, indicators of social disorganization, and other neighborhood characteristics on three substantively distinct domains of violence are also presented in Chapter 6. More specifically, the analyses in this chapter examine the effects of immigration on levels of overall, expressive, and instrumental violence. Measures of violence that include counts of non-lethal violent crimes are rare in the extant immigration literature. The results from these analyses will cast light on the extent to which immigration has a consistent impact on violence defined broadly, or if the association observed in prior research is unique to homicide. Particular attention is paid in these analyses to whether immigration has differential impacts on personal and property-based violence. Together, the results from the multivariate analyses presented in Chapter 6 will document the full range of causal effects of immigration and complement our existing knowledge regarding the relationship between immigration and violent crime.

Dependent Variables

One of the contributions of this research is that it advances current knowledge of how immigration is related to violent crimes other than homicide. As mentioned above, the present study examines the relationship between immigration and three separate indicators of violence. First, an overall measure of violent crime is used in the initial fully-specified regression models. Overall violence is an index measure that includes counts of homicides, robberies and aggravated assaults. Because such summary measures have not been included in earlier studies, researchers do not yet know whether immigration has the same predictive effect on overall violence as it does on lethal violence. Therefore, the results from these analyses are important because they are an initial test of the impact of immigration on violent crime more generally.

The remaining two dependent variables are constructed from the components of the overall violent crime measure. The second dependent variable used in this study is an indicator of expressive violence, which includes counts of homicides and aggravated assaults. The final outcome variable is a measure of instrumental violence that includes the number of robberies. Distinguishing between personal and property-based violence allows for a closer examination of whether immigration is more likely to be associated with particular types of crime. Specifically, the inclusion of a property-based measure of violence makes it possible to test directly the hypothesis that immigration is more likely to have a positive impact on neighborhood levels of financially motivated crimes (Hagan and Palloni 1999; see also Freeman 1996). Although scholars have speculated about the differential impacts of immigration, tests of this hypothesis have not been included in previous research.

Explanatory Variables

Immigration

Social disorganization theory is concerned with the impacts of exogenous forces, such as immigration, on social structure. Rather than relying solely on broad indicators of immigration, the current study includes more refined measures of a neighborhood's foreign-born population. The first is a measure of immigration that captures recency of arrival. By convention, recent immigration is defined as the number of foreign-born individuals who have been in the United States for fewer than ten years. Recent immigration has been used in prior research, particularly in the more recent neighborhood-level homicide studies (see Martinez 2002; Martinez and Lee 2000a; Lee et al. 2001).

There are substantive and theoretical reasons for including the percent recent immigrants in this study. Following the logic of the urban ecological perspective, social disorganization theory argues that over time, immigrants will assimilate into American society and are likely to experience upward occupational and residential mobility. The implication of this argument is that the size of the recent immigrant population is more likely to be associated with increased levels of violence. Although support for this hypothesis is generally not found in the empirical literature, researchers have not yet directly compared whether certain characteristics of the immigrant population have differential impacts on violence.

Additionally, this research also includes measures of immigration for specific ethnic populations. The multivariate analyses are designed to test whether levels of violence are influenced differentially by the presence of various immigrant ethnic groups. Specifically, I run four separate regression models for each city, each of which contains an ethnic-specific indicator of immigration. The ethnic immigration variable is defined as the percent of the total tract population that was born in one of the four origin countries of interest. The specific groups included in these regression models are determined by their size relative to the city's other ethnic populations. For Miami, Cubans, Nicaraguans, Hondurans, and Haitians are the city's largest ethnic groups. Similarly, models including the percent of foreign-born for Mexicans, Salvadorans, Chinese, and Vietnamese will be run for the city of Houston. Although it is the smallest city included in this study, Alexandria is unique in that it has the most diverse immigrant population. This is evidenced by the fact that the largest ethnic populations in the city have national origins from Central America, Asia, and Africa. Moreover, compared to Miami and Houston, the ten largest immigrant ethnic groups in Alexandria comprise a much smaller share of the city's total immigrant population (88.9%, 82.2%, and 53.5%, respectively). As the largest immigrant populations, Salvadorans, Ethiopians, Hondurans, and Ghanians are the ethnic groups selected for inclusion in this study (see Table 4.2).

Poverty

According to social disorganization theory, the economic deprivation of an area will be positively associated with observed levels of crime. Much of the prior research on social disorganization theory has controlled for the economic structure of an area using an absolute measure of deprivation. Researchers have constructed absolute measures disadvantage in a variety of ways; such as the percent of persons or families living below the officially defined poverty threshold, or the percent of households receiving public assistance. In the immigrant/crime literature, researchers most commonly gauge socioeconomic conditions using a measure of the percent of individuals living in poverty. Despite differences in operationalization, absolute measures of deprivation have been shown to be strong positive predictors of crimes in both immigration and non-immigration studies (see Warner and Pierce 1993; Krivo and Peterson 1996; Sampson 1987; Lee et al. 2001). To be consistent with prior immigration research, the percent of persons living in poverty is the measure of economic deprivation used in the present study.

The absolute poverty rate was selected over an alternative operationalization of economic deprivation, the gini coefficient, which has also been used in previous studies (see Peterson and Krivo 1993; Ousey 1999; Martinez 1996; Martinez 2000). The gini coefficient captures the average level of economic inequality between groups. In the more recent immigration research, the gini coefficient has been shown to be a significant predictor of homicides. For example, Martinez (1996) finds that income disparities among Hispanics are associated with increases in Hispanic homicide victimization. Further, Martinez (2000) finds that income inequality to be associated with increases in a specific type of killing, acquaintance homicides, again among Hispanics. Despite its association with lethal violence, the gini

Table 4.2. Ten Largest Ethnic Immigrant Populations by City, 2000

Total Foreign Born	Miami	%	Total Foreign Born	Houston	%	Total Foreign Born	Alexandria	%
	215,739			516,105			32,600	
Cuba	109,855	50.9	Mexico	273,567	53.0	El Salvador	5,855	18.0
Nicaragua	26,026	12.1	El Salvador	47,402	9.2	Ethiopia	2,460	7.5
Honduras	16,146	7.5	Vietnam	27,080	5.2	Honduras	1,443	4.4
Haiti	14,103	6.5	China	16,378	3.2	Ghana	1,429	4.4
Dominican Republic	7,373	3.4	Honduras	14,193	2.8	Korea	1,181	3.6
Colombia	6,826	3.2	India	13,268	2.6	Mexico	1,119	3.4
Peru	3,182	1.5	Guatemala	10,509	2.0	Other Northern Africa	1,041	3.2
Guatemala	3,093	1.4	Nigeria	7,565	1.5	Other Eastern Africa	1,015	3.1
El Salvador	2,936	1.4	Colombia	7,119	1.4	India	969	3.0
Mexico	2,182	1.0	Pakistan	6,974	1.4	Guatemala	927	2.8
Percent of all Immigrants		**88.9**			**82.2**			**53.5**

Source: Census 2000 Summary File 4.

coefficient is used primarily in studies that predict levels of race-or ethnicity-specific homicides. Because the crime data used in this study do not allow for such a disaggregation, an absolute measure of deprivation is used.

Residential Stability

Residential stability is another structural characteristic identified by social disorganization theory as having an influence on an area's ability to exercise effective social control over its residents. The measure of residential stability used in preceding analyses has been operationalized a number of different ways (see Sampson and Groves 1989; Sampson and Raudenbush 1999; Bursik and Grasmik 1993; Lee 2003). Although there is no consensus on the best construction of this measure, researchers have generally perceived residential stability as a multi-dimensional construct. In studies that include this indicator, a central aspect of this variable is concerned with residential mobility, typically defined as the percent of residents that have lived in the same dwelling for less than five years. The second component of stability generally focuses on another of the residential conditions in an area, such as the percent of owner occupied housing units or rates of housing vacancy.

The multivariate analyses conducted in this research include a measure of residential stability that is consistent with the one used in prior immigration research; one that is a combination of residential mobility and housing vacancy (see Martinez and Lee 2000a; Lee et al. 2001; Lee 2003). Specifically, this variable is constructed by first standardizing each of the component parts and then summing the derived z-scores. The resulting "instability index" reflects Shaw and McKay's (1969 [1942]) initial hypothesis that areas characterized by high levels of population turnover and vacancy will have correspondingly high levels of violent crime. Moreover, using a measure found in prior immigration research facilitates the comparability of results.

Heterogeneity

According to social disorganization theory, racial/ethnic heterogeneity will be associated with increased levels of crime because language and cultural differences impede communication and obstruct the ability to solve common problems and attain common goals (Kornhauser 1978,

p. 75). Few immigration studies include a measure of racial/ethnic diversity, despite the fact that this factor is identified by disorganization theorists as a primary source of social disruption. Specifically, to capture the degree of heterogeneity in an area, prior research has incorporated an index initially designed to measure intergroup relations (see Blau 1977; Sampson 1985; Sampson and Groves 1989; Warner and Pierce 1993).[17] The analytical models presented in this study employ the same index, calculating population diversity across four primary race/ethnic categories made available by the Census: non-Hispanic white, non-Hispanic black, Hispanic, and Asian. This measure of diversity is also more theoretically parsimonious than controlling for the size of a particular minority population (i.e., blacks).

Additional Control Variables

The analytical models used in this research also include a number of additional control variables. Prior research has shown that levels of crime are typically associated with the size of an area's population. Therefore, I control for size of the tract population in 2000, as defined by the US Census. Due to the variation in population size across tracts, this variable will be log-transformed in an effort to account for the problems associated with estimating regression models using skewed independent variables. Additionally, I control for the percentage of the population that has been shown to be at a high risk for criminal involvement (Gottfredson and Hirschi 1986). Specifically, a measure of the percent of the population who are males between the ages of 18-24 is included as a predictor of violent behavior. Controlling for the age structure of an area is common in both immigration- and non-immigration research and has been shown to be significantly related to levels of crime (see Lee et al. 2001; Lee and Martinez 2002; Peterson and Krivo 1993; Morenoff and Sampson 1997). Finally, I include a control for unemployment, measured as the percent of those aged 16 years and older in the civilian labor force who are not currently employed. Labor market participation has been shown to have an independent effect on crime, net of other measures of an area's socioeconomic conditions.

---

17 The index is calculated as $(1-\sum p_i^2)$. P_i represents the fraction of the population in a given group. Sampson and Groves (1989: 784-785) argue that this measure captures the "full range" of heterogeneity by taking into consideration both the relative size and number of race/ethnic groups.

Estimation Procedure

Analyzing patterns of violent crime across relatively small geographical areas, such as census tracts, raises a question regarding which estimation technique is best-suited for this study. It is generally accepted that the use of Ordinary Least Squares (OLS) regression procedures is not an ideal method for predicting neighborhood levels of violent crime. In part, OLS models are not favored because, as rare events, violent crimes are distributed unevenly across tracts and thus violate the OLS precondition of normally distributed indicators. The highly skewed nature of homicide distributions are such that it is difficult to establish a normal distribution even through mathematical transformation (i.e., natural logarithmic transformation). Moreover, Osgood (2000) argues that predicting tract-level homicide rates results in heteroskedastic error variances, which is another violation of OLS assumptions. Following the recommendation of Osgood (2000), I predict levels of overall, expressive, and instrumental violence using event-count regression techniques (i.e., negative binomial models). Unlike OLS techniques, event-count models do not require normally distributed dependent variables. Another advantage of event-count models is that the ratio of the parameter estimate to its standard error is t-distributed, meaning that the significance levels and magnitude of effects of the independent variables are easily determined (Osgood 2000).

Conclusion

The leading objective of this research is to examine the full range of effects of immigration on levels of violent offending. This study offers a more comprehensive view of the relationship between immigration and crime by considering the fact that immigration may impact violence through multiple causal pathways. Unlike prior research, which focuses exclusively on the direct effect of immigration on violence, the current study examines both the direct and indirect causal mechanisms through which immigration may influence violence. By modeling the indirect effect of immigration, this research casts new light on the theoretical assertion that immigration has a destabilizing, or socially disorganizing, influence on the structural composition of neighborhoods. Further, the results from the current study will document whether the lack of empirical support for disorganization theory found in the extant immigration literature is partially attributable to the methodological techniques employed in prior research. More generally, the consideration of multiple causal processes represents an analytical approach that is more consistent with the hypotheses advanced by the original social disorganization theorists, and one that will yield a more complete picture of the impact of immigration on levels of violent crime.

This research extends beyond existing research in two additional ways. The first is by predicting the impact of immigration on broadly-defined indicators of violence. To date, immigration researchers have focused almost exclusively on the relationship between immigration and lethal violence. By employing more inclusive measures of violent crime, this research offers insight into whether immigration has a consistent impact on various forms of criminal behavior (i.e., expressive vs. instrumental). Second, this research is sensitive to the fact that certain qualities of an area's immigrant population may manifest as differential impacts on levels of violence. In particular, this study examines the degree to which specific ethnic groups are more likely to be associated with higher levels of violent crime. This represents an aspect of the relationship between immigration that scholars have not yet fully investigated.

CHAPTER 5

Structural and Spatial Contexts of Violence

A primary objective of this chapter is to use descriptive statistical techniques to provide a detailed account of the neighborhood structural contexts experienced by immigrants in each of the three cities. Examining the neighborhood structural conditions of various immigrant groups represents an important initial analytical step, particularly for research on immigration, but is one that has not been widely utilized by criminologists. Disorganization theory makes clear arguments about the crime-producing effects of disrupted social structure, however, the theory does not question whether the impact of immigration on neighborhood structural factors, and in turn violent crime, is consistent across immigrant groups. The assimilationist logic of disorganization theory presupposes homogeneity among immigrants, arguing that due to their lack of skills and experience newcomers are likely to be "sorted" into similar types of neighborhoods (i.e., the zone of transition).[18] This argument was advanced by Shaw and McKay (1969 [1942]: 315) who argue that levels of crime are a product of the structural arrangement of communities, and not by their "nativity and nationality composition[s]."

Yet this hypothesis was not formally tested in the early research on disorganization theory, and it has been tacitly accepted in the more contemporary criminological research on immigration. Some of the work of immigration scholars working outside of criminology challenges the assumption that immigrants are channeled into similar types of neighborhoods. For example, Alba and Nee (1997) point out that it is increasingly common for foreigners to bypass the initial

---

18 This point is clearly articulated by Park and Burgess (1967 [1925]: 55-56) who argue that the "slums" surrounding a city's central business district are "always...crowded to overflowing with immigrant colonies."

settlement in urban enclaves, which was the common pattern for earlier European immigrant groups. Additionally, research shows that particularly over the past decade, greater numbers of recently arrived immigrants make their homes in the suburbs (see Alba et al. 1999). Taken together, these findings are suggestive of the fact that nativity may not necessarily determine residential prospects in the way ecological theory describes.

To the extent that the residential attainment patterns do not follow the classical model, it stands to reason that the relative quality of the neighborhoods into which immigrants settle may also vary by ethnicity. If immigrants are sorted into structurally dissimilar areas, this may also suggest that the effect of immigration on crime is not uniform across groups. One way to examine differences in residential outcomes is to compare the structural composition of neighborhoods inhabited by various ethnic immigrant groups. If little variation in the structural composition of immigrant neighborhoods is observed, this will be interpreted as support for the classical disorganization proposition that nativity is a primary factor in determining residential settlement patterns. By extension, such a finding may also suggest a consistency in the relationship between immigration and criminal violence across ethnic groups. However, if foreign-born ethnic groups tend to settle in qualitatively different types of places, this will indicate that the relationship between immigration and crime may not be uniform across groups. By highlighting the structural disparities in ethnic neighborhoods, the descriptive findings will also be used to inform subsequent multivariate analyses. Specifically, if large between-group differences in neighborhood structure are observed, this will underscore the importance of controlling for ethnicity to obtain a better understanding of the causal link between immigration and crime.

A second objective of this chapter is use maps to examine the spatial distributions of immigration and violence. Researchers have long been interested in how social phenomena are distributed across ecological areas. A prominent example is the work of Durkheim (1951 [1897]), who provided maps to support his arguments regarding the distribution of suicides across French departments. The scholars working out of the Chicago School of sociology also commonly used maps. In particular, urban ecologists relied on maps to describe physical organization of the city (i.e. the concentric zone model) and to document the distinct demographic composition of various areas (see Burgess 1925; Park and Burgess 1967 [1925]). Following in this tradition, two sets of maps will be presented for each city. The first series will show where the members of the four largest immigrant ethnic groups tend to settle. The visual information provided in these maps will complement the descriptive findings. Together, they will highlight not only differences in the types of places occupied by the different groups, but also how geographically isolated the largest immigrant groups are from one another.

The second set of maps will focus on the spatial distributions of criminal violence. For each city, maps of the three dependent variables of interest will be included; namely, overall levels of violent crime, as well as levels of expressive (including homicides and aggravated assaults) and instrumental violence (robberies). Because the logic of disorganization perspective suggests that the distribution of criminal behavior is not random, but rather has a distinct spatial imprint, tests of the theory have often included maps. The theoretical attention to place is even underscored by the fact that even Shaw and McKay (1969 [1942]) created dot maps to substantiate their arguments about the association between disorder and crime.

In addition to its theoretical relevance, the visual inspection of the crime patterns has methodological implications. Increasingly, criminologists are concerned with controlling statistically for the spatial dependence between areal units (see Baller et al. 2001; Heitgard and Bursik 1987; Morenoff and Sampson 1997; Cohen and Tita 1999; Griffiths and Chavez 2004). As Heitgard and Bursik (1987) claim, controlling for neighborhood interdependency is necessary to capture dynamics that often extend beyond administratively derived boundaries. Moreover, it is important to account for spatial processes in order to ensure the accuracy of the inferential statistics, and particularly to ensure that regression parameter estimates remain unbiased (Baller et al. 2001, p. 562).

The use of spatial analytic techniques has also been employed in the most recent immigration/crime research (see Lee 2003; Lee et al. 2001; Nielsen et al. 2005). For example, the work of Lee (2003; see also Lee et al. 2001) has documented a strong spatial association between local and extra-local homicide levels. Consistent with prior research, I believe the maps will show evidence of clustering, or spatial autocorrelation, operating in these data. If the visual data confirm our expectations about the "spatial nature" of crime, or they depict a clustering of violent behavior, this will suggest the need to include controls for spatial dependence in the subsequent multivariate models (Murray et al. 2001).

Descriptive Findings

In the following section, information regarding the social structural characteristics of the typical neighborhoods inhabited various nativity groups will be presented. Exposure (P*) indices are used to compare the structural conditions in the "typical" neighborhoods in each city. Although they have been more commonly employed in analyses of racial residential segregation in metropolitan areas, exposure indices are ideally suited for neighborhood-level studies (Massey and Denton 1998, 1993). Exposure indices will be computed using the following equation:

$$p^* = \frac{\sum_{i=1}^{n}(x_i * y_i)}{x_t} \qquad (1)$$

Where:
x_i=Number of group members in a tract
y_i=Neighborhood structural characteristic
x_t=Total group members in the city

Because these indices are weighted averages, they can also be used to show how "exposed" the average member of a given group is to a particular neighborhood characteristic such as poverty or unemployment (see Logan 2002). If large differences in neighborhood social structural conditions are observed, this will raise questions about whether the immigration/crime link is invariant across ethnic groups. Although this assumption is being questioned by current researchers, studies that are sensitive to the differential impact of ethnicity on crime remain scarce in the research literature (for exceptions see Martinez and Lee 1998, 2000b; Nielsen et al. 2005; Lee and Martinez 2006). An examination of neighborhood differences will cast light on how the causal relationship between immigration and crime may vary by group.

Alexandria

Compared to the total and native-born populations, foreigners living in Alexandria live in more racially/ethnically heterogeneous neighborhoods (see table 5.1). The average immigrant resides in a neighborhood that has fewer non-Hispanic whites and larger proportions of Hispanics and Asians than the typical US-born resident. In particular, the percent Hispanic accounts for the largest compositional disparities between immigrant and native neighborhoods. Whereas the average native-born individual lives in a community that is less than 13 percent Hispanic, immigrants tend to settle in areas where more than one-fifth of the population is Hispanic (21.1% for all foreigners; 23.1% recent immigrants). Although non-Hispanic blacks comprise a slightly larger share of among immigrant communities, blacks are represented at approximately the same level for all neighborhood types (ranging from 22.3% to 26.7%). In immigrant and non-immigrant neighborhoods, between 4 and 5 percent of the total population is comprised of males between the ages of 18-24.

There is a high degree of consistency between the neighborhood socioeconomic characteristics of both the total and recently arrived immigrants in Alexandria. Indeed, there are only minor differences between these groups in terms of the social structural composition of their communities. When compared to natives, however, it is clear that immigrants occupy more economically disadvantaged neighborhoods. Table 5.1 shows a sharp decline in the levels of median household between native and recent immigrant communities ($64,164 and $50,550, respectively). This pattern is consistent across other economic indicators, as the average immigrant lives in an area characterized by higher levels of poverty (11% vs. 8.4%) and unemployment (3.8% vs. 2.9%) than the typical native-born resident. Similarly, immigrants live in neighborhoods where a smaller proportion of the adult population is employed in a professional capacity (45.6% vs. 58.2%) or has graduated from college (44.1% vs. 55.9%).

Table 5.1 indicates that rates of housing vacancy are comparable in the neighborhoods of each of the groups. For native and foreign-born groups alike, unoccupied housing units comprised less than 4 percent of the total housing stock in the typical community, ranging from 3.5% (natives) to 3.8% (recent immigrants). There is little variation across communities in the proportion of recent movers, measured as the percent of householders who have lived in the same house for less than five years. Specifically, we see that both immigrants and natives live in areas where less than half of the householders have been in the same dwelling for more than five years. On average, foreigners live in areas with slightly more recent movers than natives, but the difference is

Table 5.1 Neighborhood structural characteristics for Total, Native, and Foreign-born populations, Alexandria 2000.

	Total	Native-born	Foreign-Born Total	Foreign-Born Recent
Demographic Characteristics				
% Non-Hispanic White	53.7	57.6	42.2	40.1
% Non-Hispanic Black	23.4	22.3	26.5	26.7
% Hispanic	14.7	12.6	21.1	23.1
% Asian	6.9	6.3	8.5	8.5
% Males aged 18-24	4.2	3.9	5.2	5.5
Socioeconomic Characteristics				
Median Household Income	$61,028	$64,164	$51,826	$50,550
% Poor	8.9	8.4	10.5	11.0
% Unemployed	3.1	2.9	3.7	3.8
% Professional Occupations	55.4	58.2	47.0	45.6
% College Educated	53.2	55.9	45.3	44.1
Housing Characteristics				
% Vacant Housing Units	3.6	3.5	3.7	3.8
% Recent Movers	53.8	53.7	54.0	54.6
% Homeowner	40.8	44.1	31.2	28.4
Nativity Composition				
% Foreign-Born	25.4	22.0	35.3	37.1
% Recent Immigrant	14.8	12.4	21.5	23.3

negligible (54.6% and 53.7%, respectively). We do observe a wide disparity in levels of homeownership between immigrant and non-immigrant neighborhoods. The typical foreigner resides in an area where less than one-third of the households are owner-occupied, as compared to over 44% for residents born in the United States.

Immigrants also tend to live in communities where the foreigners comprise a larger share of the total population. For example, the average immigrant lives in a neighborhood that is over 35% foreign-born, compared to an average of 22% for natives. Typically, the foreign-born also live among more recent immigrants than do natives (21.5% and 12.4%, respectively). Individuals who arrived in the US during the past decade are also settling into higher immigrant areas, as

37% of the typical recent immigrant neighborhood is foreign-born (23% recently arrived). The countries of origin for Alexandria's four largest immigrant populations are El Salvador, Ethiopia, Honduras, and Ghana. Information regarding the average neighborhood conditions for members of each of these groups is contained in Table 5.2. It is clear from this table that there are meaningful structural disparities between the neighborhoods inhabited by the Hispanic and African ethnic populations. However, the disparities in neighborhood structural conditions are less pronounced among immigrants with similar regional origins. For example, compared to the largest Hispanic immigrant groups, both Ethiopians and Ghanians have higher exposures to non-Hispanic whites and Asians. The exposure of Salvadoran and Honduran immigrants to Hispanics, on the other hand, is more than twice that of their African counterparts. Non-Hispanic blacks make-up approximately the same proportion of the total neighborhood population for each of the four ethnic groups, ranging from 23.9% (Hondurans) to 29.7% (Ethiopians). Males aged 18 to 24 are a larger proportion of Salvadoran and Honduran neighborhoods (6.3% and 7.5%, respectively), while young males represent only about 5% of the population in Ethiopian and Ghanian communities (5.1% and 5.0%, respectively).

Compared to their Hispanic counterparts, the areas inhabited by the African immigrants are less economically distressed. The neighborhoods of the typical Ethiopian and Ghanian migrants have higher median household incomes, and lower levels of poverty and unemployment than those of the Central American ethnic groups. Moreover, Honduran and Salvadoran immigrants live in areas with lower levels of college graduates and persons employed in professional occupations than the foreign-born Africans. Although the largest structural differences are found between the Hispanic and African ethnic groups, this table suggests that there are also important structural disparities between Salvadoran and Honduran communities. For example, the proportion of the population that is college educated is substantially lower in Honduran than Salvadoran immigrant neighborhoods (28.9% and 36.4%, respectively). This pattern also holds for other indicators of neighborhood quality, as foreign-born Hondurans tend to live in areas with noticeably higher levels of poverty

Table 5.2 Neighborhood structural characteristics for Ethnic Foreign-born populations, Alexandria 2000.

	Salvadoran	Ethiopian	Honduran	Ghanian
Demographic Characteristics				
% Non-Hispanic White	33.0	41.8	25.5	41.6
% Non-Hispanic Black	26.2	29.7	23.9	28.6
% Hispanic	33.3	16.3	45.5	17.5
% Asian	6.5	9.8	4.4	10.4
% Males aged 18-24	6.3	5.1	7.5	5.0
Socioeconomic Characteristics				
Median Household Income	$49,256	$47,669	$46,438	$49,297
% Poor	12.8	10.3	15.6	10.6
% Unemployed	4.6	3.7	5.6	3.4
% Professional Occupations	38.7	47.5	31.4	47.4
% College Educated	36.4	46.5	28.9	45.9
Housing Characteristics				
% Vacant Housing Units	3.2	3.6	2.4	4.5
% Recent Movers	52.3	54.6	50.9	55.0
% Homeowner	28.5	23.7	23.7	31.7
Nativity Composition				
% Foreign-Born	39.2	37.1	44.1	37.3
% Recent Immigrant	25.8	22.1	31.1	22.0

(15.6% compared to 12.8%) and unemployment (5.6% compared to 4.6%).

The results of these descriptive analyses indicate that immigrants in the city of Alexandria live in more racially/ethnically diverse and more structurally distressed neighborhoods than native-born residents. Variations in the structural composition of neighborhoods inhabited by specific immigrant ethnic groups are also observed. Among Alexandria's four largest immigrant populations, those of Hispanic origin, and particularly Hondurans, live in the most structurally disadvantaged communities. The differences in neighborhood characteristics across immigrant groups illustrate the importance of including more refined measures of immigration in criminological analyses.

Houston

In general, the foreign-born residents of Houston live in areas with a distinctly different demographic composition than natives (see Table 5.3). The exposure to Hispanics accounts for the largest differences in the racial/ethnic make-up of immigrant and non-immigrant neighborhoods. Because a majority of foreigners arrive in Houston from Mexico, Hispanics comprise nearly half of the population in the typical immigrant community. Comparatively, Hispanics are less than thirty percent of the average neighborhood population for natives. Immigrants also settle in areas with smaller proportions of non-Hispanic whites and blacks than residents born in the US. While natives live in neighborhoods that are nearly one-third non-Hispanic white (32.7%), the average for immigrant communities is only about one-quarter (25.5% for all immigrants, 24.7% for recent immigrants). Exposure to non-Hispanic blacks also varies widely by nativity, with blacks making up about 18% of the typical immigrant neighborhood, compared to 28% for natives. The size of the Asian population, as well as the proportion of males aged 18-24, are stable across neighborhood types.

Relative to native-born residents, immigrants reside in more structurally disadvantaged areas. Table 5.3 illustrates that for each of the community socioeconomic indicators, immigrant neighborhoods are dissimilar to those of American-born residents. Houston's foreign-born population lives, on average, in areas where the median household income is approximately $5,000 less than it is in native-born neighborhoods. Moreover, immigrants also live in communities with higher poverty rates, lower levels of educational attainment and professional employment. While the differences between immigrant and native communities on these latter indicators are not dramatic (ranging from about 3-5%), the results do show that the general trend is for immigrants to settle in less economically viable communities.

There are some similarities in the housing characteristics between the typical immigrant and non-immigrant neighborhoods. Table 5.3 indicates that vacancy rates stand at about 7%, regardless of nativity. There is also little variation in the levels of residential stability. Both immigrants and natives live in neighborhoods where just under half of the households are occupied by recent movers, ranging from 45.6% for natives to about 47% for immigrants. However, lower levels of homeownership characterize immigrant neighborhoods. The average native-born resident lives in a neighborhood where just over 50% of the households are owner-occupied, compared to less than 42% for the average foreigner. The difference in ownership levels is even more pronounced for recent immigrants, who live in communities where just over a third (37%) of householders own their own homes.

From Table 5.3 we observe that, compared to US-born residents, the average immigrant lives in a neighborhood where foreigners comprise a larger share of the total population. Specifically, the typical immigrant lives in an area where 35% of the population is foreign-born (37% for recent immigrants), compared to 23% for native-born residents. This pattern also extends to recently arrived immigrants who make-up about one-fifth of the population in the neighborhoods of foreign-born individuals. The typical US-born resident resides in an area where recent immigrants are less than 12% of the total population.

The residential settlement patterns in Alexandria and Houston are similar in that immigrants in both cities live in more disadvantaged neighborhoods than native-born residents. These analyses show that there are dramatic differences in the socioeconomic context of neighborhoods inhabited by immigrants in each city. Comparing poverty rates, we see that immigrants in Alexandria live in areas where about 11% of the population lives below the poverty line. Exposure to poverty is nearly twice as high for immigrants in Houston who typically live in communities where over 21% of the population is poor. Unemployment is also more prevalent in immigrant neighborhoods in Houston where over 8% of the population is out of work, compared to under 4% in Alexandria. The foreign-born in Alexandria also live in areas where more of the population is college educated and employed in professional occupations. Based on the comparisons between these cities, it appears that levels of social disorganization may be higher in immigrant communities in Houston than in Alexandria.

Over half of the foreign-born population in Houston immigrated from Mexico. Salvadoran, Vietnamese, and Chinese immigrants are the city's next three largest immigrant ethnic populations. For the Hispanic ethnic populations, we observe intra-ethnic similarities in neighborhood demographic composition (see Table 5.4). Both Mexican and Salvadoran immigrants tend to live in majority Hispanic communities (60.4% and 53.2%, respectively). Similarly, the exposure of the Hispanic ethnic groups to non-Hispanic whites is nearly identical (18.4% for Mexicans compared to 18.6% for Salvadorans). Table 5.4 shows that Mexican immigrants live in areas with relatively smaller

Table 5.3 Neighborhood structural characteristics for Total, Native, and Foreign-born populations, Houston 2000.

			Foreign-Born	
	Total	Native-born	Total	Recent
Demographic Characteristics				
% Non-Hispanic White	30.8	32.7	25.5	24.7
% Non-Hispanic Black	25.3	28.0	17.7	17.6
% Hispanic	37.4	33.2	49.0	49.7
% Asian	6.0	5.5	7.3	7.5
% Males aged 18-24	5.8	5.6	6.4	6.6
Socioeconomic Characteristics				
Median Household Income	$39,567	$40,977	$35,640	$34,267
% Poor	19.2	18.5	21.1	22.0
% Unemployed	8.1	8.1	8.2	8.2
% Professional Occupations	30.5	32.1	26.0	25.5
% College Educated	24.7	26.0	21.1	21.1
Housing Characteristics				
% Vacant Housing Units	7.6	7.7	7.4	7.7
% Recent Movers	45.8	45.6	46.3	47.6
% Homeowner	47.9	50.1	41.7	37.3
Nativity Composition				
% Foreign-Born	26.4	23.3	35.2	37.0
% Recent Immigrant	13.8	11.8	19.3	21.3

non-Hispanic black populations than Salvadorans (16.6% compared to 21.0%), while the latter live in areas with larger Asian populations (6.8% compared to 4.2%). Although the typical Vietnamese and Chinese immigrant is exposed to Asians at similar levels (15.6% and 16.5%, respectively), the overall racial/ethnic composition of their neighborhoods vary. Relative to their Chinese counterparts, Vietnamese immigrants live in areas with larger Hispanic (37.1% compared to 28.3%) and non-Hispanic black (20.3% compared to 17.1%) populations. However, Chinese immigrants are exposed at higher levels to non-Hispanic whites (37.6% compared to 26.5%). The percent of males aged 18 to 24 is consistent across each of the ethnic communities.

Table 5.4 Neighborhood structural characteristics for Ethnic Foreign-born populations, Houston 2000

	Mexican	Salvadoran	Vietnamese	Chinese
Demographic Characteristics				
% Non-Hispanic White	18.4	18.6	26.5	37.6
% Non-Hispanic Black	16.6	21.0	20.3	17.1
% Hispanic	60.4	53.2	37.1	28.3
% Asian	4.2	6.8	15.6	16.5
% Males aged 18-24	6.8	6.7	5.6	5.4
Socioeconomic Characteristics				
Median Household Income	$31,124	$31,766	$37,856	$44,741
% Poor	24.2	23.2	17.7	16.5
% Unemployed	9.4	8.6	7.4	6.0
% Professional Occupations	18.9	21.6	28.9	42.0
% College Educated	13.2	16.5	23.3	39.2
Housing Characteristics				
% Vacant Housing Units	7.4	7.3	6.5	7.0
% Recent Movers	43.0	46.6	47.8	50.4
% Homeowner	42.9	37.2	45.5	40.4
Nativity Composition				
% Foreign-Born	37.0	38.8	36.0	34.9
% Recent Immigrant	20.0	22.0	19.1	20.1

The two Hispanic immigrant ethnic groups live in more disadvantaged neighborhoods than their Asian counterparts. The average median household income in both Mexican and Salvadoran communities is approximately $31,000, while Vietnamese and Chinese immigrants tend to live in areas where the household income is more than $37,000 and $44,000, respectively. Comparing the other dimensions of social structure suggests that the Hispanic ethnic groups live in areas characterized by higher levels of disadvantage. Typically, Mexicans and Salvadorans reside in neighborhoods where nearly one-quarter of the population is poor (24.2% and 23.2%, respectively). Rates of neighborhood poverty are lower for the Asian immigrant groups, ranging from 17.7% for Vietnamese to 16.5% for Chinese.

Levels of exposure to college educated and professionally employed individuals are generally higher in Asian ethnic neighborhoods. This is particularly true for Chinese immigrants who tend to settle in areas where nearly 40% of the population holds a college degree and 42% are professionally employed. In the average Mexican neighborhood, on the other hand, only about 13% of the population is college educated and less than 20% are employed in a professional or managerial capacity.

The typical neighborhood occupied by members of the four largest immigrant ethnic groups has similar housing characteristics. For example, vacancy rates stand at about 7% in the typical ethnic immigrant neighborhoods (ranging from 6.5% for Vietnamese to 7.4% for Mexicans). Although the overall levels are comparable, there is more variation in levels of residential stability across foreign-born ethnic communities. Mexican immigrants occupy neighborhoods with the lowest rates of instability (43%), while the typical Chinese community has the largest proportion of recent movers (50.4%). Homeownership is most prevalent in Mexican and Vietnamese communities where 42.9% and 45.5% of householders own their homes, respectively. The average Salvadoran and Chinese immigrants live in neighborhoods with ownership rates of 37.2% and 40.4%, respectively.

The neighborhoods inhabited by members of the largest ethnic groups have similar nativity compositions. Each of the immigrant ethnic groups has similar levels of exposure to foreign-born persons. As Table 5.4 indicates, in the communities into which members of the largest immigrant groups settle, foreigners make-up approximately 35% to 39% of the total population. The presence of recent immigrants is also consistent across ethnic neighborhoods, as between 19.1% and 22.0% of their populations have been in the US for fewer than ten years.

Miami

Unlike the two cities discussed above, the majority of Miami's population is Hispanic (66%). This population characteristic is reflected in the large Hispanic presence in the overall neighborhood racial/ethnic composition between nativity groups (see Table 5.5). US-born residents live in communities in which Hispanics account for nearly one-half of the population (49.2%). In the typical immigrant neighborhoods, the proportion of Hispanics increases to over 75%.

Exposure to Asians is very low for both native and foreign-born residents, averaging less than one percent of the population in their respective communities. Similarly, immigrants and US-born residents typically do not live in areas with large shares of non-Hispanic whites. From Table 5.5 we observe that that natives tend to live in areas where whites represent only about 13% of the population and the value does not exceed 12% for immigrants. The size of the non-Hispanic black population does vary widely between immigrant and non-immigrant communities. Indeed, the exposure to blacks for US-born residents is over three times the level experienced by immigrants.

Of the three cities under investigation, Miami's neighborhoods are the most socioeconomically disadvantaged. From Table 5.5 we observe that the average Miami resident, regardless of nativity, lives in a community that is more economically distressed than those in Alexandria or Houston. Comparing median household incomes, we see that the neighborhood values in Miami are less than half the levels of corresponding neighborhoods in Alexandria ($26,719 to $61,028 for natives, $25,375 to $51,826 for all immigrants). Further, average household incomes in Houston average from $10,000 to $15,000 higher than corresponding values in Miami. This pattern is consistent for other economic indicators, as the typical US- and foreign-born residents of Miami also live in areas characterized by much higher poverty and unemployment rates. Taken together, these descriptive results suggest that neighborhoods in Miami are generally more disadvantaged than the communities in the other cities under investigation. The differences in neighborhood quality also mirror the variations in the overall levels of violent behavior between these cities.

Despite their relatively higher levels of disadvantage, the typical immigrant and native-born neighborhoods are more structurally similar in Miami than they are in the other cities. American-born residents live in communities where the average median household income values exceed those in immigrant communities by only $2,000. There are also only modest differences in neighborhood poverty and unemployment rates. Table 5.5 shows that approximately 27% of population in the average immigrant neighborhood lives in poverty, compared to 31% for US-born residents. It is worth noting that immigrants have lower levels of exposure to poverty and unemployment than natives. In the typical immigrant and native communities, exposure to unemployment ranges from 12% to 14% for immigrants and natives, respectively. On average, both immigrants and non-immigrants occupy neighborhoods

Table 5.5 Neighborhood structural characteristics for Total, Native, and Foreign-born populations, Miami 2000.

	Total	Native-born	Foreign-Born Total	Recent
Demographic Characteristics				
% Non-Hispanic White	11.8	13.1	10.9	10.7
% Non-Hispanic Black	21.3	36.4	11.0	11.6
% Hispanic	65.8	49.2	77.0	76.6
% Asian	0.9	0.9	0.9	0.9
% Males aged 18-24	4.5	4.7	4.5	4.6
Socioeconomic Characteristics				
Median Household Income	$25,919	$26,719	$25,375	$24,741
% Poor	28.7	31.3	26.9	27.8
% Unemployed	12.5	13.8	11.6	11.9
% Professional Occupations	21.0	22.7	19.8	19.3
% College Educated	15.2	16.2	14.6	14.3
Housing Characteristics				
% Vacant Housing Units	8.5	10.8	7.0	7.1
% Recent Movers	39.5	40.4	38.9	39.5
% Homeowner	34.7	35.1	34.4	32.2
Nativity Composition				
% Foreign-Born	59.5	46.9	68.1	68.0
% Recent Immigrant	22.3	17.6	25.5	26.4

where less than 25% of the population is college educated or employed in professional occupations.

Table 5.5 also shows that nativity is not associated with large disparities in neighborhood housing characteristics. Miami's native-born residents tend to live in areas characterized by slightly higher vacancy rates than immigrants (11% compared to 7%). Although the differences are small in magnitude, fewer households are occupied by recent movers in the average immigrant neighborhoods (39% compared to 40%). There are similarly small differences in levels of homeownership in the typical neighborhoods of immigrant and US-born residents (34% and 35%). The communities into which recent immigrants settle have the lowest ownership rates (32%).

Consistent with the pattern observed in the other two cities, Miami's foreign-born residents tend to live in areas with larger immigrant populations. On average, immigrants in Miami reside in neighborhoods where over two-thirds of the population was born abroad. Further, immigrants tend to settle in areas where recent immigrants account for more than 25% of the population. In the communities of non-immigrants, less than half of the population is foreign-born and nearly 18% arrived in the US within the last decade.

More than half (51%) of Miami's immigrant population was born in Cuba. Indeed, there are more than four times as many Cubans as Nicaraguans, the city's second largest immigrant ethnic group (12.1%). Hondurans and Haitians are the next largest ethnic groups making up 7.5% and 6.5% of all immigrants, respectively. There are a number of similarities in terms of the community demographic characteristics for these groups, despite the large disparities in population size (see Table 5.6). Typically, the foreign-born members of each of these ethnic groups live in neighborhoods that are less than 10% non-Hispanic white and approximately 1% Asian. Also, members of these groups reside in areas where young adult males average between 4% and 5% of the total population.

The largest differences in the racial composition of the immigrant ethnic neighborhoods are found in the exposures to non-Hispanic blacks and Hispanics. The average Cuban, Nicaraguan, and Honduran immigrant settles in an area where more than 75% of the population is Hispanic, compared to only 24% for Haitians. Conversely, foreign-born Haitians live in areas averaging more than 65% non-Hispanic black. In the average Cuban and Nicaraguan neighborhoods, non-Hispanic blacks make up less than 5% of the total population (3.5% and 4.7%, respectively). Hondurans have a higher exposure to non-Hispanic blacks, but they still tend to settle in neighborhoods where blacks are less than 11% of the total population.

Not only are Cubans the largest immigrant ethnic group in Miami, but they also tend to live in the least economically distressed neighborhoods (see Table 5.6). For example, the poverty rate in the neighborhood of the typical Cuban immigrant is between six and twelve points lower than in the communities of the other groups. Median household incomes are also more than $4,000 higher in the typical foreign-born Cuban community. Continuing this trend, we see that Cuban immigrants tend to settle in areas with the lowest rates of unemployment and the highest levels of professional employment and educational attainment. From Table 5.6 we also observe that the

Table 5.6 Neighborhood structural characteristics for Ethnic Foreign-born populations, Miami 2000.

	Cuban	Nicaraguan	Honduran	Haitian
Demographic Characteristics				
% Non-Hispanic White	9.8	8.0	9.7	9.0
% Non-Hispanic Black	3.5	4.7	10.9	65.5
% Hispanic	85.8	86.4	78.2	24.0
% Asian	0.8	0.7	1.0	1.0
% Males aged 18-24	4.2	4.8	4.9	5.2
Socioeconomic Characteristics				
Median Household Income	$25,685	$21,469	$21,258	$21,032
% Poor	24.3	30.0	32.1	36.9
% Unemployed	10.7	12.6	13.5	16.0
% Professional Occupations	19.3	14.9	16.5	16.3
% College Educated	14.1	10.6	11.5	9.9
Housing Characteristics				
% Vacant Housing Units	5.2	5.9	7.4	13.1
% Recent Movers	37.5	39.9	40.9	39.4
% Homeowner	37.9	26.6	25.6	29.9
Nativity Composition				
% Foreign-Born	73.0	73.7	67.4	45.0
% Recent Immigrant	26.5	29.0	26.9	18.0

average Nicaraguan and Honduran immigrants live in neighborhoods with similar socioeconomic compositions. It should also be noted that Haitian immigrants tend to live in areas with the highest levels of disadvantage across each of the dimensions of neighborhood socioeconomic status.

Comparing housing characteristics provides further evidence that there are distinct differences in the types of neighborhoods inhabited by members of the four largest immigrant groups. For example, Cubans settle in areas where nearly forty percent of households are owner-occupied (37.9%), while homeownership rates average less than 30% for the other groups. The neighborhood of the typical Cuban immigrant also tends to be more residentially stable. Cuban immigrants tend to live in areas where 37.5% of the population has lived in the same home for less than five years, compared to about 40%

for foreign-born Nicaraguans, Hondurans, and Haitians. With the exception of Haitians, members of the largest immigrant populations live in communities where between 5% and 7% of all housing units are vacant. Haitians have the highest exposure to housing vacancy, living in areas where over 13% of homes are unoccupied.

Immigrants of Hispanic origin reside in areas with similar nativity compositions. The typical Cuban, Nicaraguan, and Honduran immigrants reside in neighborhoods where over two-thirds of the population is foreign-born (73.0%, 73.7%, and 67.4%, respectively). Further, members of these immigrant groups settle in communities where more than 25% of the population is recent immigrants (26.5%, 29.0%, and 26.9%, respectively). However, Haitian immigrants settle in areas where less than half of the total population is foreign-born (45.0%) and less than one-fifth of the population immigrated within the last decade (18%).

The descriptive analyses have provided important information on a number of issues relevant to this research. First, the results discussed above demonstrate that there is variation in the social structural characteristics in the neighborhoods across cities. Generally speaking, residents of Alexandria live in communities that are the least economically distressed, while those in Miami live in areas with the highest levels of disadvantage. These descriptive findings do offer some support for social disorganization theory, as the relative levels of neighborhood disadvantage correspond to the overall violent crime rates in these cities. Specifically, in 2000, the violent crime rate in Alexandria was the lowest of the three cities under investigation, while corresponding rates in Houston and Miami were dramatically higher.[19] Although previous immigration research has recognized the regional differences in levels of offending, existing studies have not included comparisons of the average social structural characteristics across the areas under investigation (Lee et al. 2000; Martinez 1996).

Of particular salience to this study, the neighborhood comparisons also illustrate that there are clear differences in the structural composition of neighborhoods inhabited by different immigrant ethnic populations. The fact that ethnic populations reside in areas with varying levels of disadvantage suggests that that the association between immigration and crime may differ as a product of ethnicity.

---

19 Violent crime rates for the year 2000 were calculated using counts of crimes known the police provided by the FBI's Uniform Crime Reports (http://www.fbi.gov/ucr/ucr.htm).

The fact that there are important differences among the foreign-born population is one that has been well established in the urban research literature, but one which has been generally overlooked by criminologists (Alba et al. 1999; Portes and Rumbaut 2001). In doing so, contemporary criminological researchers have partially accepted disorganization theory's proposition which emphasizes the similarity of immigrants, and therefore assumes a uniformity in the effect of immigration on crime (for an exception see Martinez and Lee 1998, 2000b). For the purposes of the multivariate modeling, these findings demonstrate the importance of introducing measures of ethnicity, rather than focusing primarily on the recency of arrival.

Spatial Distributions

We now turn to the spatial distributions of immigration and violent criminal behavior. For each of the cities, a map showing the neighborhoods containing the highest concentrations of the four largest immigrant ethnic groups will be presented. The visual data on immigration will provide a broad overview of whether there are similarities in the settlement patterns of immigrants across cities. To the extent that immigrants are more geographically dispersed in one city than another, the maps will highlight such differences. A second series of images, which compare the distributions of the dependent variables of interest, will also be included. Specifically, the crime maps will display the spatial distributions of the overall, instrumental, and expressive crime rates. Examining the distributions of violent crime will help to assess whether the concentrations of violence violate the assumption of spatial randomness (see Baller et al. 2001).

The maps are created using Exploratory Spatial Data Analysis (ESDA), a technique that examines local indicators of spatial association (LISA). In particular, the maps presented in this chapter are based on a localized version of the Moran's I statistic, commonly referred to as the Moran scatterplot (Anselin et al. 2000, p. 232-233). Moran scatterplot maps have a number of characteristics them make them better suited for the exploration of spatial patterns than traditional mapping techniques. First, Moran scatterplot maps provide information about the strength of the spatial autocorrelation for a given distribution. Rather than relying on simple visualization techniques, LISA methods identify clusters using a sampling distribution to determine significant deviations from spatial randomness (Baller et al. 2001; Cohen and Tita 1999). Second, such maps also offer information regarding the direction of the observed spatial autocorrelation. In computing the local moran statistics, positive (or negative) associations are determined by comparing local values on a particular variable to values at neighboring locations (see Baller et al. 2001, p. 570). Because they provide "an intuitive means to visualize the degree of spatial autocorrelation," the scatterplot maps are an ideal tool for examining the spatial distributions of immigrant groups and violent criminal behavior (Anselin et al. 2000, p. 233).

While spatial analysts have identified several distinct forms of spatial dependence, the maps presented in this chapter focus on a specific form of clustering; namely, areas where the high values on the variables of interest concentrate geographically.[20] The clustering of high values is of particular relevance to this study because the theoretical discussions of geographic concentration appear to be concerned with this spatial phenomenon. For example, disorganization theory argues that due to limited residential options, many immigrants will be channeled into neighborhoods that are in close proximity to one another. That is, the theory holds that areas with the highest concentrations of immigrants are likely to congregate geographically. The theory makes similar claims about how high-crime areas tend to be found in close proximity to one another. Therefore, to determine whether the distributions of immigration and violent crime follow theoretical expectations, the maps will show the clustering of high values. As mentioned previously, an added benefit of the crime maps is that they will confirm whether it will be necessary to include a control for spatial dependence in the regression analyses (see Anselin et al. 2000).

Alexandria

Alexandria has a racially diverse immigrant population, which accounts for nearly thirty percent of the city's 128,000 residents. In Figure 5.1, we see that the largest immigrant groups tend to settle in geographically distinct areas of the city.[21] Salvadoran immigrants, who are the largest ethnic immigrant group in the city, are concentrated in neighborhoods

---

20 Conditions of positive spatial autocorrelation are identified as "high-high" clusters on the Moran scatterplot maps. See Baller et al. (2001) for a description of the other forms of spatial clustering.

21 Note that according to ESDA criteria, there were no neighborhoods in which the concentration of Hondurans met the minimum threshold to be considered a spatial cluster.

in the northern portion of the city. Nearly 46% of foreign-born Salvadorans live in the three neighborhoods identified as part of the Salvadoran cluster. The neighborhoods with the highest concentrations of African immigrants are found in the western area of the city. Substantial portions of the largest African immigrant groups are concentrated spatially, as over two-thirds of all of Ghanian and Ethiopian immigrants live within their respective ethnic neighborhood clusters. Geographically, foreign-born Ethiopian and Ghanian neighborhoods are in close proximity to one another, although the majority of these immigrant populations do not reside the same communities. Clearly this should not be taken to suggest that there are no communities shared by members of both groups. This finding does indicate, however, that there are no areas where the presence of both groups is sufficient enough to be considered a "mixed" ethnic neighborhood.

Figure 5.2 presents the spatial distributions of criminal violence in Alexandria. It is important to note that the rates of violent crime in Alexandria fall well below the national averages. For example, using crime data for 2000, the violent crime rate in the city is about 271 offenses per 100,000 persons, compared to the national average of 474 per 100,000.[22] A similar pattern is also observed when the overall violent crime rate is decomposed into its instrumental and expressive components. Specifically, rates of expressive violence are approximately 145 compared to the national average of 330 per 100,000, while comparable levels of instrumental violence are 126 for the city and 145 nationally. Keeping in mind the relatively low levels of crime in city, the maps will allow for an examination of how these events concentrate geographically.

The first map on Figure 5.2 shows the clustering of overall violent crime rates. We see from this image that four neighborhoods are identified as having higher than expected levels of violence. A cluster of three adjacent neighborhoods combines to form a larger grouping in the southeastern portion of the city, and another high-violence area is located to the north of this larger cluster. Interestingly, this same collection of neighborhoods is distinguished as having high concentrations of instrumental violence. From Figure 5.2 we can see that heaviest concentrations of interpersonal violence are found in two neighborhoods that are a subset of the larger overall violence cluster.

---

22 Rates do not include counts of forcible rapes.

Figure 5.1 Spatial Clustering of Ethnic Immigrant Neighborhoods,
Alexandria 2000.

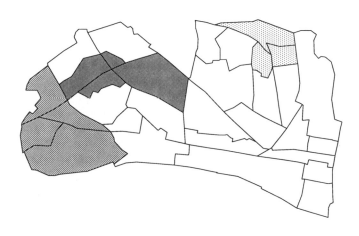

Salvadoran Neighborhoods
Ghanian Neighborhoods
Ethiopian Neighborhoods
City of Alexandria

Figure 5.2 Spatial Clustering of Overall Violent Crime Rates, Expressive Crime Rates, and Instrumental Crime Rates, Alexandria, 2000.

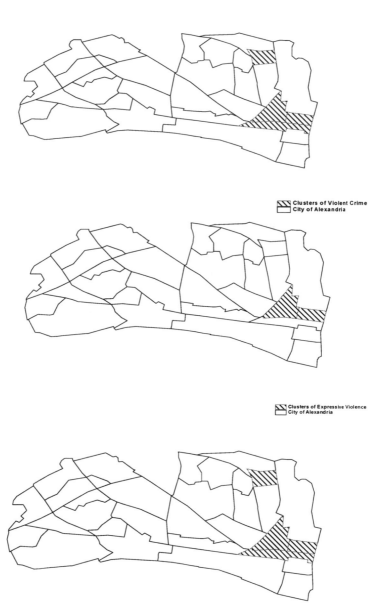

As disorganization theory expects, the visual data do suggest that violent criminal behavior is concentrated disproportionately within a limited number of geographical areas.

A value of the Moran scatterplot maps is that they show the locations neighborhoods with significant concentrations of violent crime. However, the visual data alone do not provide information regarding the empirical distinctiveness of these areas in terms of their levels of crime. A closer look at the violent crime rates within these communities will offer some perspective on whether levels of crime in these areas are substantively different from those observed for the city as a whole. Indeed, the violent crime rate in these areas is 687 per 100,000, a level more than twice the city rate. Similarly, the rate of expressive violence in these tracts is 437 per 100,000, which exceeds the city average of 145 by a wide margin. Property-based violent behavior among the clustered neighborhoods further confirms the exceptionally high levels of violence in these communities compared to the city (247 and 126 per 100,000, respectively). Not only are the levels of violence in these areas high relative to the city totals, they are also higher than their respective national averages.

A visual inspection of the communities with the highest levels of violent crime in Alexandria provides support for the theoretical assertion regarding the distribution of crime across ecological areas. Although the patterns are not perfectly compatible, the evidence suggests that areas with the highest levels of criminal violence are located in close proximity to one another. Similarly, a closer examination of these areas reveals that, as the theory holds, absolute levels of crime are substantially higher in these areas than they are for the city as a whole. More generally, the spatial patterns observed in the maps do suggest that the rates of violent crime in Alexandria may be spatially autocorrelated.

Houston

Although immigrants comprise similar percentages of the total populations in Houston and Alexandria (26.4% and 25.3%, respectively), Houston is home to a far greater number of foreigners. In 2000, more than half a million of Houston's residents were foreign-born, meaning there were nearly sixteen times as many immigrants in Houston than Alexandria. Being located in a border state, the immigrant population in Houston is disproportionately Hispanic, with over half (53%) of the city's foreign-born population being of Mexican descent. In Figure 5.3 we see that Mexican immigrants settle in two primary areas of the city, indicated by the large cluster of Mexican neighborhoods north of the city center and another to the south and east. There are two smaller Mexican communities extending to the east and northwest of the city center. Approximately 54% of the foreign-born Mexicans reside in one of the 85 (of 518) tracts determined to have significant concentrations of Mexican immigrants. It is also interesting to note that, with very few exceptions, Mexican immigrants do not tend to settle in areas also occupied by members of the other large immigrant groups. To the extent Mexican immigrants live in mixed ethnic communities, the neighborhoods are shared with Salvadorans.

Salvadorans comprise over nine percent of Houston's immigrant population. The heaviest concentrations of Salvadoran neighborhoods are found in the southwest area of the city. Much of the Salvadoran immigrant population lives in neighborhoods clustered among other co-ethnic immigrant communities. Similar to Mexicans, nearly half of the foreign-born Salvadorans (48%) live in one of the 48 neighborhoods with a significant concentration of co-ethnics. The primary cluster of Salvadoran communities is found within the large "mixed ethnic" cluster located near the western edge of the city, where nearly one-quarter of foreign-born Salvadorans live.[23] It is somewhat difficult to detect from the map, but the results from this analysis reveal that substantial portions of Houston's largest immigrant groups do not settle in geographically distinct areas. In addition to having significant Salvadoran representation, most of the neighborhoods within this overlapping cluster are also identified as both Vietnamese and Chinese immigrant communities. Immigrant settlement patterns in Houston appear to be very different than those in Alexandria. In the former we see that many of the ethnic immigrant communities appear to be racially/ethnically heterogeneous, including sizable Hispanic and Asian populations.

Nearly three-quarters of the Vietnamese immigrants live in one of several clusters of ethnic neighborhoods dispersed across the city. Although Vietnamese immigrant communities are found in different areas of the city, half of all foreign-born Vietnamese residents settle

---

23 "Mixed ethnic" neighborhoods are those that are identified through the LISA process as belonging to a "high-high" cluster of more than one ethnic immigrant group. Such neighborhoods are identified here because they suggest that some groups may be more likely than others to settle into ethnically heterogeneous areas.

Figure 5.3 Spatial Clustering of Ethnic Immigrant Neighborhoods, Houston 2000.

Mixed Ethnic Neighborhoods
Mexican Neighborhoods
Salvadoran Neighborhoods
Vietnamese Neighborhoods
Chinese Neighborhoods
City of Houston

Figure 5.4 Spatial Clustering of Overall Violent Crime Rates, Expressive Crime Rates, and Instrumental Crime Rates, Houston, 2000.

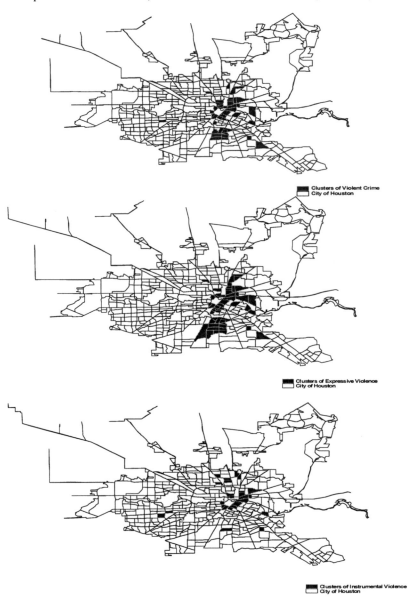

in one of the heterogeneous neighborhoods described above.   In addition to the large ethnically mixed immigrant cluster, Vietnamese immigrants are heavily concentrated in two other regions, one located in the southeastern portion of the city and another in the northwest. Both of these clusters are similar in that they do not contain any ethnically mixed neighborhoods.   Compared to their Vietnamese counterparts, a smaller percentage of Chinese immigrants live in largely co-ethnic neighborhoods. Specifically, a large share of Chinese immigrants (37%) resides in ethnically mixed neighborhoods. However, less than 20% of the foreign-born Chinese settle in ethnic communities outside of this large heterogeneous cluster.

Compared to Alexandria, levels of criminal violence in Houston are much higher.   Indeed, due to its high crime rates, the city has been recognized as one of the hundred most violent in the country.[24] Between 1999 and 2001, the overall violent crime rate in the city was more than twice the national average (1,089 and 474 per 100,000, respectively).   The same is true for Houston's rates of expressive and instrumental violence, both of which are more than 300 points higher than the corresponding national rates.[25]   Of particular interest to this research, however, is the spatial pattern associated with the high overall rates of violence. In order to gain a sense of the spatial dispersion of violence in Houston, maps depicting the distributions will be discussed below. Again, the visual data are used mainly as a tool to illustrate the extent to which violent criminal behavior is geographically concentrated.

As expected, the maps demonstrate a high degree of spatial association among the neighborhoods with the highest levels of violence (see Figure 5.4).   The map of overall violent crime rates shows a primary cluster of neighborhoods that encompasses the downtown area and extends both northward and southward from the city center. Similarly, the distribution of expressive violence is nearly identical to the spatial imprint observed for overall rates. With few exceptions, areas with the highest concentrations of interpersonal violence also tend to be the most violent generally.   However, as is evident in the third map, the rates of instrumental violence are distributed slightly differently.   Specifically, we see that instrumental violence is

---

24 http://www.morganquitno.com/cit02a.pdf
25 The expressive crime rate in Houston is over 636 per 100,000 compared to
    330 per 100,000 for the nation. Similarly, the instrumental crime rate in the
    city is approximately 452 per 100,000 compared to the national average of
    145 per 100,000.

distributed more narrowly, that is, there are fewer neighborhoods identified as having significant concentrations of property-based violence. Still, the distribution of instrumental violence is similar to the other crime measures in that all are located in the same general areas of the city.

As mentioned previously, a limitation of these maps is that they fail to provide substantively important information about the observed levels of violence within the clustered areas. To better understand the uniqueness of such areas in terms of their levels of violence, it will again be instructive to compare the rates of violence in the clustered neighborhoods to the city totals. As was the case in Alexandria, these areas are distinguished by their high levels of violence. The overall violent crime rate for the forty-one high crime neighborhoods is over 1,100 points higher than the city rate (2,257 and 1,089 per 100,000, respectively). Similarly, the rate of property-based violence among these neighborhoods is 884, a level significantly higher than the city rate of 452 per 100,000. Levels of expressive violence also surpass the comparable city rate by a large margin (1469 and 636 per 100,000, respectively). The exceptionally high rates of crime among this collection of tracts, as well as the visual evidence provided by the maps provide strong evidence that levels of violent crime in Houston are spatially dependent.

Miami

Of the cities being studied, immigrants make up the largest share of the total population in Miami, where nearly 60% of all residents were born outside of the United States. A map showing the concentrations of the specific ethnic populations reveals that over half (56%) of Miami's neighborhoods have meaningful representations of one of the four largest immigrant ethnic groups (see Figure 5.5). Similar to the pattern observed in Alexandria, Figure 5.5 indicates that foreign-born ethnic groups largely settle in geographically distinct regions of the city. In other words, ethnically heterogeneous communities are less frequent in Miami than they were in Houston. With the exception of 5 tracts, neighborhoods with significant concentrations of immigrants were represented by only one of the four largest ethnic groups.

The majority of immigrants arrive in Miami from Cuba. Given that they comprise about 51% of the city's immigrant population, the largest cluster of immigrant neighborhoods has significant concentrations of by Cuban-born individuals. Over one-quarter of

Miami's neighborhoods are identified as having high concentrations of foreign-born Cubans. The cluster of Cuban neighborhoods is located west of the downtown area. Together, the 22 neighborhoods where Cuban immigrants tend to settle form a single large cluster that is adjacent to the city's western boundary. Not only does this cluster cover a wide geographic area, it is also home to a majority of the foreign-born population. Specifically, over 62% of all Cuban immigrants reside in one of these clustered neighborhoods. From this map, we also see that no Cuban neighborhood is also associated with another ethnic immigrant group.

Nicaraguans are the second largest foreign-born ethnic population in Miami, representing about 12% of all foreigners. The map reveals a distinct settlement pattern for the foreign-born Nicaraguans. Nicaraguan immigrants are likely to settle near the center of the city, just west of downtown and east of the Cuban immigrant communities. There are eight tracts that comprise this cluster of neighborhoods, in which approximately 45% of Nicaraguan immigrants live. Foreign-born Nicaraguans tend to settle in neighborhoods in close proximity to both Cuban and Honduran communities. Interestingly, despite this geographic propinquity, very few neighborhoods have a mixed ethnic composition. To the extent that there are ethnically mixed areas, it occurs between Nicaraguans and Hondurans. In addition to the mixed ethnic communities, the cluster of Honduran neighborhoods includes three additional tracts that extend northward. Compared to Nicaraguans, Honduran immigrants have a lower likelihood of settling in a predominantly co-ethnic community, as only 31% of Hondurans born abroad live in one of these clustered Honduran neighborhoods.

There is a single cluster of Haitian immigrant neighborhoods in Miami, a collection of ten tracts located in the northeastern area of the city. When the spatial distributions of these groups are compared, the evidence suggests that settlement patters are not determined solely by nativity, but that they may also be influenced by the race of the immigrant group. This is indicated by the fact that Haitian immigrant communities are not located in close proximity to the clusters of the Hispanic immigrant neighborhoods. Not only are Haitian immigrants more geographically isolated from the other groups, they also have an increased likelihood of residing in a co-ethnic neighborhood. Whereas between 30-60 percent of Cuban, Nicaraguan, and Honduran immigrants live in

Figure 5.5 Spatial Clustering of Ethnic Immigrant Neighborhoods, Miami 2000.

Figure 5.6 Spatial Clustering of Overall Violent Crime Rates, Expressive Crime Rates, and Instrumental Crime Rates, Miami, 2000.

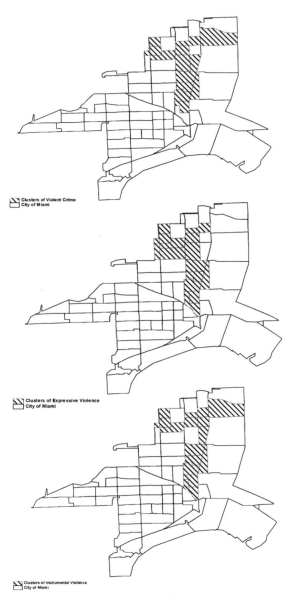

co-ethnic neighborhoods, over three-quarters of Miami's foreign-born Haitian population lives in a neighborhood with a significant concentration of foreign-born Haitians.

Violent crime rates for the city of Miami, and particularly homicide rates, have consistently ranked among the nation's highest over the past decade (see Lee et al. 2001). For example, between 1999 and 2001 Miami averaged nearly 2,000 violent crimes committed per 100,000 of the population, a rate more than four times the national average. Differences in the comparable levels of expressive violence are similar, with the rates in Miami exceeding those for the nation by 800 points (1130 and 330 per 100,000, respectively). The disparity is even more pronounced for robbery rates, which are nearly six times higher in Miami than they are for the country (869 and 145 per 100,000, respectively). To obtain a clearer understanding of how these various types of violence are distributed spatially, maps will again be used. A benefit the visual summary is that inconsistencies in the spatial patterning of the different measures of violence will be easily detected.

Considering the clustering of violence observed in the other two cities, it comes as little surprise that the maps reveal a similar pattern in Miami. Specifically, the spatial data indicate that the city's high overall crime rates are largely driven by a few neighborhoods characterized by disproportionately high levels of violence (see Figure 5.6). The map of overall violent crime rates shows that there are roughly fifteen neighborhoods identified as having significant concentrations of violence. Interestingly, all of the neighborhoods are adjacent to one another and together form a single cluster that extends northward from the downtown area. Similar to the patterns observed in the other cities, the distributions of both expressive and instrumental violence follow the overall pattern very closely. Consistent with the findings discussed above, rates of violence within this cluster are dramatically higher than the corresponding city values. Indeed, rates of violent, expressive, and instrumental crimes among these tracts are more than twice as high as the city averages (5,185, 3,176, and 2,009 per 100,000, respectively).

Conclusion

The goal of this chapter was to provide an overview of the comparable structural conditions and the spatial patterning of violence for each of the cities in this study. In some ways, the analyses conducted in this chapter were confirmatory, rather than exploratory, in nature. For example, the findings from the descriptive analyses indicate that differences among the foreign-born population have implications for residential attainment possibilities. Put more simply, the results demonstrate that ethnic immigrant groups are not sorted into structurally equivalent neighborhoods. These results are not entirely unexpected, as the differential settlement patterns of ethnic groups, particularly in recent years, is a phenomenon that has been documented by urban scholars (see Alba et al. 1999; Alba and Nee 1997). Nevertheless, the findings discussed here still make an important contribution to criminological research. Specifically, these results make clear the importance of including measures of ethnicity to understand more completely the relationship between immigration and crime.

ESDA procedures were also used to analyze the spatial distributions of violence. As a growing body of research has established, it is important to test and to control for the potentially biasing influences of spatial autocorrelation (Baller et al. 2001). As Anselin et al. (2000) contend, Moran scatterplot maps provide a key initial test for the presence of spatial clustering. As expected, the crime maps presented for each of the cities did support the notion that areas with the highest concentrations of criminal violence tend to be spatially concentrated. Because the visual inspection confirmed expectations, controls for the underlying spatial dependence will be included in the multivariate models to be discussed in the next chapter.

CHAPTER 6

Direct and Indirect Effects of Immigration on Violence

In this chapter I examine the full range of effects of immigration on levels of violence. For the purposes of this study, there are two mechanisms through which immigration may affect violent criminal conduct; namely, indirect and direct causal channels. Recall that a central tenet of disorganization theory is the belief that immigration will have a deleterious impact on the social order of neighborhoods. That is, the theory perceives immigration as a disruptive, or "disorganizing" social process. More specifically, disorganization theory proposes that the influence of immigration on crime will be indirect, operating through its impact on neighborhood social structure. Following the theoretical logic, the disorganization perspective holds that in the multivariate analyses, neighborhood social structure will mediate much of the overall impact of immigration on violence.

By contrast, many of the conclusions drawn in the growing body of immigration/crime literature cast doubt on this proposition. Inconsistent with the expectations of classical disorganization theory, the work of Martinez and colleagues consistently finds that immigration predicts lower levels of violence (Martinez 2002; Martinez and Lee 1998, 2000a; Lee et al. 2001; Lee 2003). The negative direct effect of immigration on violence, and particularly lethal violence, is typically interpreted as an inability of disorganization theory to account for the relationship between immigration and crime in a contemporary social context. Although this inverse direct association certainly suggests a complexity to the relationship between immigration and crime that disorganization theorists may not have anticipated, it is not clear whether this finding completely invalidates the original theoretical arguments. The conclusions drawn in much of the existing research are limited, in part, because the methodology on which they are based does not allow for such a broad assessment of the theory. I submit that drawing from more recent immigration scholarship, there are reasons to expect that immigration may influence violence through both direct and indirect causal pathways (see Kao and Tienda 1995; Portes and Rumbaut 2001). It is hoped that by considering both processes, this research will cast additional light on some of the intricacies of a relationship that is still not well understood by criminologists.

It will be clear how the results from the descriptive analyses are used to inform decisions regarding the multivariate models. In the previous chapter, the findings from the comparison of neighborhood characteristics demonstrate that there are distinct differences in the structural quality of neighborhoods inhabited by various ethnic groups. It is this finding that underscores the importance of testing for ethnic differences in the relationship between immigration and crime. Similarly, based on the examination of the spatial distributions of violence, the maps clearly document that the concentrations of crime in each city violate the assumption of spatial randomness. To control for the geographic clustering of violent criminal behavior, spatial lags will be included in the fully-specified regression models.

Estimating the full range of effects of immigration on violence cannot be done using a single multivariate regression equation. Instead, a series of regression models designed to capture specific components of this relationship will be estimated. The discussion in this chapter will be separated into two sections, each of which provides findings for the conceptually distinct components of the relationship; 1) the impact of immigration on social structure, and 2) the impact of immigration on violence. In the first section, I will present a set of tables that focus on the impacts of immigration on the structural factors associated with social disorganization. Ordinary Least Squares (OLS) regression techniques are used to estimate the effect of immigration on poverty, racial/ethnic heterogeneity, and residential instability. The second section presents the results from the analyses that predict violence. Due to the highly non-normal distributions of the dependent variables, event-count methods (i.e., negative binomial regressions) are used to predict the effect of immigration and other neighborhood factors on violence (see Osgood 2000). Taken together, the results from this multi-stage approach will offer a perspective on the relationship between immigration and crime that is not available from prior studies.

Before moving to the discussion of the initial multivariate results, it should be noted that the measures of violence used in this study differ from those used in pervious analyses on this topic. Rather than focusing exclusively on the effect of immigration on lethal violence, the current study employs a more comprehensive set of outcome variables (see Martinez 1996; Martinez 2000; Lee 2003). Specifically, the multivariate results presented in the final section will discuss the effects of immigration on three different measures of violence. The first is an overall measure of violence, which includes counts of homicides, robberies and aggravated assaults. Including this broader measure of violence is important because it represents an initial examination of the relationship between immigration and violence broadly defined. Violence is further subdivided into two substantively distinct categories depending on whether the crime may have been financially motivated. The measure of property-based (instrumental) violence includes counts of robberies, while that for person-based (expressive) violence includes counts of homicides and aggravated assaults.[26]

Differentiating between instrumental and expressive violence has relevance to this research because scholars have hypothesized that immigration is likely to be associated with increased levels of property crime (see Hagan and Palloni 1999). Specifically, Hagan and Palloni contend that because many immigrants arrive in the US with limited occupational prospects, some may use the underground economy to improve their financial situation.[27] This is not to say that all activities associated with the informal, or underground economy are criminal in nature, only that illicit opportunities may be used by some immigrants to help soften their transition into American society. Although the claim by Hagan and Palloni raises an interesting theoretical question, it has not been formally tested in prior research. More generally, using broader definitions of violence will complement our existing knowledge regarding the extent to which immigration influences observed levels of criminal deviance. Despite the fact that the results presented here are not directly comparable to those presented in the existing literature, it is hoped that the benefit of using more inclusive

---

26 The use of this categorization follows Maume and Lee (2003: 1144-1145) who argue that the instrumental/expressive dichotomy remains a useful distinction for macro-level violence research.

27 For a complete discussion of the "foraging" model described by Hagan and Palloni (1999), see Freeman (1996).

measures of violence will be a gain in insight into theoretically relevant questions that have yet to be fully addressed by criminologists.

Effects of Immigration on Social Structure

This section presents the results from regressions which test whether immigration has a disruptive, or disorganizing effect on the social structural composition of neighborhoods. For each city immigration will be used to predict the three dimensions highlighted by disorganization theory as the most likely to be associated high levels of crime: poverty (percentage of persons living below poverty line), residential instability (an index constructed by adding z-scores of the percentage of vacant buildings and the percentage of residents who resided in a different location in 1995), and heterogeneity (an index that captures overall levels of racial/ethnic diversity). Because these proxies for disorganization are used in the second stage regression models, for the sake of comparability, these indicators are operationalized according to definitions established by prior criminological research on immigration. To review, the use of the absolute measure of poverty and the instability index follow directly from earlier studies (Martinez and Lee 1998, 2000a; Lee et al. 2001). The diversity index employed in this research, although it has not been widely used in prior immigration studies, addresses the theoretical notion of heterogeneity by considering both the relative size and the number of race/ethnic groups in a given neighborhood (see Sampson and Groves 1989; Warner and Pierce 1993; see also Blau 1977).

Before discussing the results from the initial OLS regressions, it should be noted that the primary goal of the following analyses is not to capture the full array of factors that may be associated with neighborhood levels of poverty, residential instability, and diversity. Instead, these models focus specifically on a theoretically informed, though incomplete relationship; namely, the effect of immigration on social structure. Certainly there are factors other than immigration, not included in the analytical models, which are likely to influence the social structural characteristics of neighborhoods. However, it is not entirely clear what factors should be included as predictors of social structural conditions. Although measures of poverty, residential stability, and diversity are typically conceptualized as independent variables, in the initial regressions presented in this chapter, they are included as dependent variables. Model selection is further complicated by the fact that prior cross-sectional research has not established a standard set of controls for structural conditions. The results presented in the following tables are based on bivariate analyses. The inclusion of bivariate regressions has limitations, among them is the fact that it may difficult to assess immigration's true impact on neighborhood social structure. However, the values reported in the tables are interpreted here in much the same way correlation coefficients; that is, although they are instructive of the relationship underpinning the variables of interest, they must be interpreted with some caution

In more practical terms, given the levels of immigration into these three cities, it stands to reason that the presence of foreigners has had a measurable impact on the structural composition on the neighborhoods into which they settle. For example, the size of the foreign born populations in Alexandria and Houston increased dramatically over the past decade, growing by more than 75% in each city (81.1% and 77.7%, respectively). Similarly, 40% of the foreign-born population in Miami has been in the US for less than a decade. It stands to reason, then, that immigration will have tangible impacts on neighborhood social structure, as disorganization theory hypothesizes. Yet it is also important to recognize that by omitting other explanatory variables, the following models provide only a partial picture of the factors that influence the structural composition of communities.

Alexandria

Among the various foreign-born populations in Alexandria we observe many similarities in their impacts on neighborhood social structure (see Table 6.1). For example, the results in Table 6.1 indicate that there is a positive and significant association between immigration and poverty.[28] Foreign-born Ethiopians are the exception to this trend, as the presence of this ethnic group is not related to high levels of poverty. Another consistent pattern that emerges from this analysis is the effect of immigration on neighborhood demographic composition. Specifically, we see that the size of the foreign-born population, both the general (% recent arrivals) and specific (ethnicity) measures, contributes to neighborhood heterogeneity. The effects are strongest for the two African immigrant ethnic groups, but given the diversity of the

---

28 All p-values presented in this chapter are based on 2-tailed tests of significance.

Table 6.1 Effects of immigration on Neighborhood Social Structure by Nativity, Alexandria 2000.

	Poverty			Residential Instability			Diversity		
	β	Beta	R²	β	Beta	R²	β	Beta	R²
Recent Immigration	0.246 **	0.523	0.250	-0.027	-0.179	0.032	0.012 ***	0.687	0.454
Ethnic Groups									
Salvadoran	0.430 **	0.470	0.195	-0.082	-0.280	0.048	0.013 *	0.363	0.103
Ethiopian	0.634	0.307	0.064	-0.126	-0.190	0.036	0.044 ***	0.560	0.291
Honduran	0.874 *	0.413	0.143	-0.185	-0.271	0.043	0.007	0.082	0.007
Ghanian	1.849 *	0.418	0.147	0.007	0.010	0.010	0.113 ***	0.674	0.436

immigrant population in Alexandria, the positive relationship is not entirely surprising. Of the immigrant groups under investigation, only Hondurans did not have a significant impact on neighborhood racial/ethnic composition. An interesting pattern is that immigration is not systematically related to levels of neighborhood instability.[29]

The results for Alexandria offer partial support for the disorganization theory's claims that immigration may have a disruptive influence on community social structure. The fact that immigration predicts higher levels of both poverty and racial/ethnic diversity is consistent with theoretical expectations. Despite the overall consistency in the results, we see that the impact of immigration on social structure is not uniform across groups. This finding not only challenges the theoretical claims, but also reinforces the notion that it is important for criminologists to move beyond the treatment of immigrants as a single conceptual category. Nor do the results for Alexandria provide support for the disorganization perspective's argument that immigration facilitates residential instability.

Houston

In Houston, the impact of recent immigration on social structure is similar to the pattern observed for Alexandria. In Table 6.2 we see that

---

29 In all the models for recent immigrants, the mobility component of the residential instability index was adjusted so that it did not include the number of recent immigrants.

Table 6.2 Effects of immigration on Neighborhood Social Structure by Nativity, Houston 2000.

	Poverty			Residential Instability			Diversity		
	β	Beta	R²	β	Beta	R²	β	Beta	R²
Recent Immigration	0.457 **¹	0.334	0.110	-0.016 *	-0.092	0.007	0.006 ***	0.282	0.078
Ethnic Groups									
Mexican	0.491 **¹	0.483	0.232	-0.038 ***	-0.299	0.088	0.000	-0.018	0.011
Salvadoran	1.398 **¹	0.261	0.066	-0.085 **	-0.128	0.014	0.021 ***	0.260	0.066
Vietnamese	-0.376	-0.074	0.005	-0.050	-0.079	0.006	0.033 ***	0.434	0.187
Chinese	-1.333 **¹	-0.146	0.019	0.012	0.011	0.012	0.030 ***	0.222	0.047

areas with higher proportions of recent immigrants are also those with correspondingly high levels of poverty and racial/ethnic diversity. One noticeable difference between the cities is that recent immigration in Houston is associated with residential instability, although not in the expected direction. Specifically, these results show a negative relationship between the proportion of recent arrivals and the residential instability index, suggesting that immigrants are not channeled into residentially unstable areas. Although statistically significant, the association between immigration and residential instability is not a strong one, as indicated by the fact that recent immigration explain only a small portion of the variance in residential instability (R^2=.01).

The results for the ethnic-specific models show comparable patterns to those observed for recent immigrants. For example, Table 6.2 shows that the size of the Salvadoran, Vietnamese, or Chinese population is associated with high levels of neighborhood diversity. Based on a comparison of the standardized coefficients and explained variance, the Vietnamese immigrants have the strongest influence on the racial composition of neighborhoods. This finding also confirms a point that was suggested in the descriptive analyses that foreign-born Vietnamese tend to live in more heterogeneous communities than the other ethnic immigrant groups. The size of the Mexican immigrant population is not related to diversity, which again suggests that members of this group are more likely to live in co-ethnic neighborhoods.

Of Houston's four largest immigrant populations, only the two Hispanic groups have a statistically significant impact on residential stability. Consistent with the relationship observed for recent immigrants, there is an inverse association between the size of the Mexican and Salvadoran populations and the residential stability index. Table 6.2 also shows that the impact of immigration on the socioeconomic structure of neighborhoods varies as a product of ethnicity. Specifically, the positive relationship between Mexican and Salvadoran immigrants and poverty indicates that poverty rates tend to be the highest in the areas where members of these ethnic groups are the most prevalent. However, this pattern does hold for Vietnamese and Chinese immigrant populations, both of which are associated with lower levels of poverty. Between the Asian ethnic groups, the size of the Chinese immigrant population has the stronger negative impact on poverty, although the effect for Vietnamese immigrants approaches the level of statistical significance (t =1.68, p<.09).

The Houston analysis shows mixed support for disorganization theory's assertion that immigration has a disorganizing influence on social structure. The significant positive effects of immigration on both poverty and racial/ethnic heterogeneity conform to theoretical expectations. Disorganization theory clearly articulates that the arrival of immigrants should have negative structural consequences. However, the findings for Houston do not support the hypothesis that immigration is a residentially destabilizing force. To the extent that immigration is significantly associated with neighborhood turnover, the size of the foreign-born population predicts *lower* levels of instability. More generally, these results again illustrate that the relationships between immigration and social structure are not uniform across groups. The differences between ethnicities point out the limitations of treating immigrants as a unified population, an issue that has been long recognized by urban scholars (Alba et al. 1999; Alba and Nee 1997).

Miami

In some ways, the results for the city of Miami are distinctly different from those discussed above. In Miami, recent immigration is associated with lower levels of neighborhood poverty, while in the other cities we observed significant positive effects (see Table 6.3). As the largest immigrant ethnic group, the effect of recent immigration on poverty appears to be driven by the size of the foreign-born Cuban population. Different from the other ethnic groups included in the current analysis, Cubans are shown to have a very strong negative

Table 6.3 Effects of immigration on Neighborhood Social Structure by Nativity, Miami 2000.

	Poverty			Residential Instability			Diversity		
	β	Beta	R²	β	Beta	R²	β	Beta	R²
Recent Immigration	-0.431 **	-0.329	0.096	-0.094 ***	-0.637	0.398	-0.010	-0.071	0.010
Ethnic Groups									
Cuban	-0.338 **'	-0.540	0.282	-0.047 ***	-0.670	0.441	-0.010 **	-0.356	0.115
Nicaraguan	-0.252	-0.132	0.010	-0.104 ***	-0.479	0.219	-0.008 **	-0.330	0.097
Honduran	0.308	0.100	0.010	-0.081 *	-0.232	0.041	0.010	0.050	0.010
Haitian	0.312 *	0.244	0.047	0.015	0.105	0.011	0.011 *	0.268	0.059

effect on community poverty rates. The presence of Nicaraguan immigrants is also inversely related to poverty, although this relationship is not statistically significant. Nor are poverty rates causally linked to the size of the Honduran foreign-born population. Of the four primary immigrant groups, only Haitians have a positive effect on neighborhood poverty rates. This latter finding squares with theoretical expectations and prior research that has documented that Haitians generally arrive in this country with few financial resources. As Portes and Zhou (1994: 19) describe, many Haitians "sell everything in order to buy passage to America" (see also Portes and MacLeod 1996).

The results from this analysis do not lend support to the disorganization theory's assertion that immigration facilitates residential instability. Regardless of which measure of immigration is included in the models, only negative or null effects are found. Specifically, areas with larger shares of recently arrived foreigners, as well as those where more Cubans, Nicaraguans, and Hondurans settle are not characterized by high levels of instability. Comparing the standardized coefficients and explained variances, these results indicate that the size of the foreign-born Cuban population has the strongest residentially stabilizing influence of Miami's primary ethnic groups. This finding is consistent with the patterns observed in Houston, where immigration was also found to be associated with lower levels of residential turnover.

There are mixed findings for the effects of immigration on the racial/ethnic composition of neighborhoods. In both Alexandria and

Houston, the evidence suggests that levels of diversity are influenced by the size of the foreign-born population. This pattern is replicated for Haitians immigrants in Miami, who contribute significantly to higher levels of diversity. Yet the same relationship is not observed for the other primary immigrant ethnic populations. Table 6.3 reveals that the size of the recent immigrant population is unrelated to community heterogeneity. However, these results indicate that there is a negative relationship between the size of the Cuban and Nicaraguan immigrant population and the racial/ethnic composition of neighborhoods. Put another way, of Miami's four largest ethnic groups, Cuban and Nicaraguan immigrants tend to promote the homogenization, rather than the racial/ethnic diversity, of communities.

The theoretical proposition regarding the disorganizing effects of immigration is not well supported by the initial regression models run for Miami. In most cases, when immigration is found to have a significant impact on social structure, the direction of the relationship is negative. Instead of exerting a disruptive influence, as social disorganization theory expects, immigration in Miami is associated with lower levels of structural disadvantage. The strength of the negative relationships is strongest for Cubans, an immigrant population that has established a strong ethnically-identified community (see Wilson and Portes 1980; Portes and Rumbaut 2001). The results for Haitians are most consistent with the disorganization perspective's claims, as the presence of this group is associated with high levels of both poverty and racial/ethnic heterogeneity. However, the results for Haitians are the exceptions to the overall pattern observed in Miami. The more consistent finding for Miami, as was the case in the other cities, is that the effect of immigration on social structure varies across groups.

Effects of Immigration and Neighborhood Factors on Violence

The second set of regression results focuses on the effects of immigration and neighborhood structural factors on violence. Again, because the dependent variables are measured as the number of observed violent events in a given neighborhood, the regression equations are run using the negative binomial estimation procedure (see Osgood 2000). Although the size of the population is typically included as an independent variable in linear regression estimation procedures, event-count methods control for population size differently. The accepted practice is to include the natural logarithm of the population as an "offset" in the regression statement and to assign it a fixed coefficient of one, effectively transforming the regression into "an analysis of rates of events per capita" (Osgood 2000, p. 27). Because the counts of violent crimes are rare events, the data used here also satisfy the requirement that the offset variable is 10 to 100 times greater than the event count variable to ensure that a negative binomial distribution is approximated (see Liao 1994: p. 70-72).

To obtain a better understanding of how immigration impacts levels of violence, three separate models are run for each of the foreign-born populations by city. For each group, the first column shows the results from the equation that predicts violence using the disorganization variables and the neighborhood controls. The purpose of this initial equation is to establish that the data used in this study are able to replicate patterns observed in previous research. The effect of immigration on lethal violence, net of the neighborhood controls, is shown in the second column. The third column is the fully-specified model, which includes measures of immigration, social disorganization, and other neighborhood factors including a control for spatial dependence.[30]

Particular interest will be paid in this discussion to a comparison of the size and strength of the immigration coefficient between the second and third models. As mentioned previously, a critique of contemporary criminological research on immigration is that it is not sensitive to the notion that immigration may have countervailing effects on levels of criminal behavior. Instead, researchers have focused exclusively on the direct effects, ignoring the possibility that immigration may be linked crime through its impact on neighborhood social structure (see Martinez 2000a, 2002; Lee 2003; Lee et al. 2001). Changes in the immigration coefficient between the second and third models will shed some light on this question. If the coefficient for immigration remains relatively unchanged in both models, in terms of the effect size and/or the strength of association with criminal violence, this will suggest that the effect is operating independently of the other variables in the

---

30 Following Tolnay et al. (1996: 796-799) the spatial term included in the models is created using a two-stage estimation procedure. In the first step, a set of predicted values are created by regressing the dependent variable on all of the independent variables of interest. These fitted values were then transformed into a spatial weighted average using the SpaceStat statistical software package (Anselin 2001). It is this resulting weighted average that is included in the second stage regressions as the control for spatial autocorrelation.

model. However, attenuation in the size and/or predictive strength will suggest that social structure has a mediating influence on the relationship. Unlike prior studies, this research attempts to document whether immigration may influence levels of criminal violence through multiple causal channels. Following a brief discussion of the correlation matrices, the regression results will be discussed separately for each city.

Correlations

Tables 6.4 to 6.6 present the city-specific bivariate correlations for the independent variables to be included in the regression models. It is common to review the correlation structures as a first attempt to assess the degree to which multicollinearity among the independent variables may result in biased parameter estimates in the multivariate analyses (see Land et al. 1990; Warner and Roundtree 1997). By convention, correlations that have absolute values of .80 and greater are thought to be problematic for the purposes of multiple regression. Although we observe that there are three correlations greater than .70, none exceed the .80 threshold. Specifically, in Alexandria, there is a correlation of .72 between percent recent immigrants and percent males aged 18-24. In both Houston and Miami, there are similarly high correlations between poverty and unemployment (.71 and .73, respectively). Additional diagnostics will be conducted in the subsequent multivariate analyses, but the results from the correlations do not reveal that there may be unacceptable levels of multicollinearity in any of the models.

Multivariate Results

Alexandria

The first table presents the results from the regressions predicting overall levels of violent crime (see Table 6.7). As is evident in Table 6.7, there are many similarities in the results across each of the immigrant groups. With respect to the structural factors associated with disorder, we see that, for each group, poverty emerges as a significant predictor of levels of violent crime in the baseline (Model 1) and fully-specified models (Model 3). This finding comes as little surprise, as the consequences of economic deprivation on levels of

Table 6.4 Correlations of Independent Variables, Alexandria 2000.

	1	2	3	4	5	6	7	8	9	10
1 % Recent Immigrants	1									
2 % Honduran Immigrants	0.46	1								
3 % Salvadoran Immigrants	0.65	0.85	1							
4 % Ethiopian Immigrants	0.63	-0.10	0.04	1						
5 % Ghanian Immigrants	0.67	-0.07	0.12	0.56	1					
6 % Poverty	0.52	0.41	0.47	0.31	0.42	1				
7 Diversity Index	0.69	0.08	0.36	0.56	0.67	0.61	1			
8 Instability Index	0.16	-0.12	-0.06	0.02	0.23	0.29	0.24	1		
9 % Males aged 18-24	0.72	0.47	0.63	0.44	0.47	0.60	0.68	0.09	1	
10 % Unemployed	0.43	0.41	0.50	0.29	0.09	0.47	0.37	-0.01	0.38	1

Table 6.5 Correlations of Independent Variables, Houston 2000.

	1	2	3	4	5	6	7	8	9	10
1 % Recent Immigrants	1									
2 % Mexican Immigrants	0.70	1								
3 % Salvadoran Immigrants	0.65	0.44	1							
4 % Vietnamese Immigrants	0.27	-0.04	0.21	1						
5 % Chinese Immigrants	0.23	-0.19	0.08	0.29	1					
6 % Poverty	0.33	0.48	0.26	-0.07	-0.15	1				
7 Diversity Index	0.29	-0.01	0.26	0.43	0.22	-0.17	1			
8 Instability Index	0.13	-0.17	0.02	-0.02	0.07	0.01	0.26	1		
9 % Males aged 18-24	0.33	0.35	0.24	-0.01	-0.04	0.29	0.18	0.31	1	
10 % Unemployed	0.08	0.31	0.10	-0.06	-0.17	0.71	-0.20	0.02	0.37	1

Table 6.6 Correlations of Independent Variables, Miami 2000.

	1	2	3	4	5	6	7	8	9	10
1 % Recent Immigrants	1									
2 % Cuban Immigrants	0.61	1								
3 % Nicaraguan Immigrants	0.72	0.43	1							
4 % Honduran Immigrants	0.55	0.11	0.69	1						
5 % Haitian Immigrants	-0.10	-0.49	-0.35	-0.25	1					
6 % Poverty	-0.33	-0.54	-0.13	0.10	0.24	1				
7 Diversity Index	-0.07	-0.36	-0.33	0.05	0.27	-0.06	1			
8 Instability Index	-0.41	-0.58	-0.31	-0.07	0.07	0.51	0.36	1		
9 % Males aged 18-24	0.08	-0.20	0.11	0.15	0.25	0.20	0.15	0.14	1	
10 % Unemployed	-0.32	-0.39	-0.12	0.08	0.14	0.73	-0.07	0.42	0.32	1

criminal deviance has been well established in both the immigration and non-immigration research literature (see Warner and Pierce 1993; Krivo and Peterson 1996; Sampson 1987; Lee et al. 2001). Also consistent with theoretical expectations, we see that levels of neighborhood instability are associated with higher levels of violence. The exceptions to this trend are seen in the models for recent immigrants and Ethiopians, where population turnover is not related to observed levels of violence. Further, in three of the five final models, we observe that neighborhood demographic composition is linked to violence; however, the association is not in the anticipated direction. Contrary to expectations, areas that are more racially/ethnically diverse tend to have lower levels of violence.

Next to levels of poverty, unemployment is the most consistent predictor of overall violent crime in Alexandria. As hypothesized, levels of participation in the formal labor market have a positive impact on levels of criminal violence. While poverty and unemployment are clearly conceptually interrelated, there is no evidence that including both as independent predictors in the models produced biased estimates due to multicollinearity (see Land et al. 1990). Using the Variance Inflation Factor (VIF) model diagnostic, there was no indication of bias due to a high inter-correlation among the independent variables; namely, none of the VIF values exceeded the conventionally accepted threshold of 4.0.[31] Additionally, net of other neighborhood factors, the age structure of neighborhoods does not contribute much to our understanding of the causes of violence in Alexandria. Nor does the control for spatial dependence emerge as a significant predictor of overall levels of violence. This latter finding is somewhat surprising given that strong spatial relationships have been observed in prior criminological research (see Baller et al. 2001; Lee 2003; Nielsen et al. 2005; Lee et al. 2001). Because Alexandria is comprised of relatively few neighborhoods (32 tracts), it is possible that the lack of spatial dependence is an artifact of the small number of neighborhoods on which the lagged term is based.

Our attention now shifts to the relationship between immigration and violence. The following discussion focus on changes in the size (and magnitude) of the immigration coefficient between the second and third models for each group. The behavior of this coefficient across models is important because it will indicate the extent to which

---

31 Similar diagnostic tests were run for each of the models presented in this chapter and no evidence of multicollinearity was discovered.

Table 6.7 Negative Binomial Regression of Violent Crime on Immigration and Neighborhood Structural Factors, Alexandria 2000.

	Recent Immigrant			Salvadoran			Ethiopian			Honduran			Ghanian		
	(1)	(2)	(3)	(1)	(2)	(3)	(1)	(2)	(3)	(1)	(2)	(3)	(1)	(2)	(3)
Social Disorganization															
Poverty	0.09 **	--	0.06 **	0.09 **	--	0.09 ***	0.09 **	--	0.09 ***	0.09 **	--	0.09 ***	0.09 **	--	0.09 ***
Diversity	-1.28 **	--	-1.66 **	-1.28 **	--	-1.18 *	-1.28 **	--	-0.91	-1.28 **	--	-1.20 *	-1.28 **	--	-0.87
Residential Instability	0.08	--	0.09	0.08	--	0.10 *	0.08	--	0.07	0.08	--	0.09 **	0.08	--	0.09 **
Immigration	--	0.01	-0.01	--	0.04	0.03	--	-0.06	-0.07 *	--	0.06	0.04	--	0.06	-0.13 *
Control Variables															
Unemployment	0.21 ***	0.27 **	0.16 **	0.21 ***	0.20 *	0.16 **	0.21 ***	0.27 **	0.19 ***	0.21 ***	0.23 **	0.17 **	0.21 ***	0.28 **	0.17 ***
Males Aged 18-24	-0.05	0.03	0.08	-0.05	0.00	-0.09	-0.05	0.10	-0.01	-0.05	0.04	-0.06	-0.05	0.06	0.00
Spatial Lag	--	--	0.08	--	--	0.06	--	--	0.06	--	--	0.08	--	--	0.07
Intercept	-6.62 ***	1.16 **	-7.98 ***	-6.62 ***	1.43 ***	-7.20 ***	-6.62 ***	1.13 ***	-7.44 ***	-6.62 ***	1.34 ***	-7.53	-6.62 ***	1.07 ***	-7.55 ***

N^a (32)

* $p < .05$, ** $p < .01$, *** $p < .001$

Note: Dependent variable is the average annual count of homicides, aggravated assaults, and robberies between 1999-2001.

[a] Calculations are based on the same number of tracts are in each model

social structure has a mediating influence on the relationship between immigration and crime. The results in Table 6.7 do not show a consistent association between the size of a foreign-born population and overall levels of violence. For three groups (recent immigrants, Salvadorans, and Hondurans), the size of the foreign born population has no meaningful impact on violence, as the effects fail to reach levels of statistical significance.

For the remaining two groups, the size of the ethnic-specific immigrant population is significantly related to levels of violence. In the fully-specified models for both of the Ethiopians and Ghanians, we see that the presence of these foreign-born ethnic populations has a negative impact on criminal violence. Interestingly, for both groups, the direct effect of immigration is significant only in the final models. This result suggests that the causal influence on violence for these groups operates independent of social structure, a finding consistent with much of the prior research on this topic (see Sampson and Bean 2006; Martinez 2002; Martinez and Lee 1998; Lee et al. 2001). However, because the negative direct effect is observed for only two of the groups, these results offer only limited support for the notion that immigration influences crime through two distinct causal pathways.

In addition to examining its impact on violence generally, this research is also concerned with how immigration may be related differentially to specific types of crime. Again, the focus on expressive and instrumental violence is designed to test a hypothesis advanced by Hagan and Palloni (1999), which proposes that immigration will have opposite impacts on the two domains of criminal behavior. The following tables contain the results from the first multivariate analyses designed to test this hypothesis empirically. To the extent that the results show that immigration is negatively association with levels of expressive violence, and positively related to instrumental crime, this will be interpreted as support for the Hagan and Palloni hypothesis. Such a finding would also highlight the importance of distinguishing between types of crime in future criminological studies of immigration.

Before moving to a discussion of the multivariate results, it will be instructive to describe generally the specific distributions of expressive and instrumental violence in Alexandria. For the period under investigation, the Alexandria Police Department documented nearly the same number of expressive and instrumental crimes. Specifically, between 1999 and 2001, the official department records contained information on a total of 350 violent criminal acts, of which 186 (53%) of the crimes were expressive and 164 (47%) were instrumental in nature. Interestingly, these proportions differ considerably from national averages, where expressive crimes comprise a much larger share of all violent acts known to the police (approximately 70% and 30%, respectively).[32] Despite Alexandria's parity in expressive and instrumental offending, this does not necessarily suggest that there will be little variation in the impact of immigration on the different expressions of violence. The distributions are mentioned here in order to provide some background on how the patterns of violence in Alexandria differ from national trends.

The results from the regressions predicting levels of expressive and instrumental violence are presented in Table 6.8 and Table 6.9. These results are discussed together because there are a number of similarities between the results from these analyses and those for overall levels of violence. In both tables we again see that poverty is a strong and robust predictor of violence, while the other neighborhood factors associated with social disorganization are largely unrelated to observed levels of crime. For example, the residential instability index does not predict higher levels of expressive violence and is only associated with higher levels of instrumental violence in two instances. As we see in Table 6.9, population turnover is only associated with higher levels of property-based violence in the Salvadoran and Ghanian models. The relationship between the racial/ethnic composition of neighborhoods and levels of violence also tends to be negative, although the pattern of association is not as clear as it was for overall levels of violent criminal conduct. Other than for recent immigrants, neighborhood diversity predicts significantly lower levels of instrumental violence only in the Ethiopian model. The results from these models again show mixed support for the disorganization theory. As expected, neighborhood economic deprivation has a strong positive impact on levels of criminal violence. However, in a broader view, the findings from these regressions fail to support the theoretical claim that each of the indicators of disorganization will contribute uniquely to higher levels of violence.

The effects of the other control variables are also largely consistent with those observed in the models predicting overall levels of violent crime. Again we see that unemployment is linked to higher levels of both   expressive   and   instrumental   violence   in   all   but   two

---

32 National ratios are based on UCR data for the year 2000 and include only
    the offense categories used in these analyses
    (http://www.fbi.gov/ucr/cius_00/xl/00tbl01.xls).

Table 6.8 Negative Binomial Regression of Expressive Violence on Immigration and Neighborhood Structural Factors, Alexandria 2000.

	Recent Immigrant			Salvadoran			Ethiopian			Honduran			Ghanian		
	(1)	(2)	(3)	(1)	(2)	(3)	(1)	(2)	(3)	(1)	(2)	(3)	(1)	(2)	(3)
Social Disorganization															
Poverty	0.11 ***	--	0.06 **	0.11 ***	--	0.13 ***	0.11 ***	--	0.11 ***	0.11 ***	--	0.13 ***	0.11 ***	--	0.12 ***
Diversity	-1.24 *	--	-1.58 *	-1.24 *	--	-0.80	-1.24 *	--	0.11	-1.24 *	--	-0.77	-1.24 *	--	-0.59
Residential Instability	0.08	--	0.08	0.08	--	0.10	0.08	--	0.06	0.08	--	0.09	0.08	--	0.09
Immigration	--	0.00	-0.01	--	0.04	0.03	--	-0.12	-0.14 *	--	0.05	0.04	--	0.10	-0.10
Control Variables															
Unemployment	0.26 ***	0.37 ***	0.16 *	0.26 ***	0.30 **	0.20 **	0.26 ***	0.35 ***	0.23 ***	0.26 ***	0.33 **	0.21 ***	0.26 ***	0.39 ***	0.22 ***
Males Aged 18-24	-0.08	0.06	0.08	-0.08	-0.01	-0.12	-0.08	0.11	-0.03	-0.08	0.03	-0.09	-0.08	0.04	-0.03
Spatial Lag	--	--	0.14	--	--	0.21 *	--	--	0.16	--	--	0.26 *	--	--	0.20
Intercept	-7.65 ***	0.14	-8.00 ***	-7.65 ***	0.46	-8.99 ***	-7.65 ***	0.18	-9.12 ***	-7.65 ***	0.33	-9.36	-7.65 ***	0.07	-9.23 ***
N[a]	(32)														

* p< .05, ** p< .01, *** p < .001

Note: Dependent variable is the average annual count of homicides and aggravated assaults between 1999-2001.

[a] Calculations are based on the same number of tracts are in each model

models. It should be noted that in both instances where unemployment was not associated with violence (Salvadoran and Honduran models, Table 6.9), the relationships approach levels of statistical significance (p<.07 and p<.09, respectively). These results again find neighborhood age structure to be unrelated to levels of violence. Similarly, these results generally do not show that the spatial dependence has a unique impact on expressions of either personal- or property-violence. The two exceptions to this trend are both found in Table 6.8, where we see that observed levels of expressive violence are influenced by levels in surrounding neighborhoods only in the Salvadoran and Honduran models.

Disaggregating the Alexandria crime data into expressive/instrumental categories does not reveal that immigration has differential impacts on particular forms of violence. Indeed, the findings illustrate that in most cases immigration does not have a direct influence on either expressive or instrumental violence. In these tables we observe that that only in a single model (Ethiopian model, Table 6.8), does the size of the foreign-born ethnic population impact levels of violence. While the direction of the relationship is negative, the more general lack of association between immigration and specific measures of violence in Alexandria offers little support for the notion that immigration may have countervailing influences on crime.

Given the expectations of disorganization theory, one somewhat surprising result was the consistent negative effect of diversity on violence. A possible explanation for this finding is that, as Warner and Pierce (1993:509) argue, racially homogeneous neighborhoods, particularly those occupied by African-Americans, are likely to be characterized by high levels of crime because they are both socially isolated and unable to provide "access to legitimate opportunity structures."

To examine whether a strong racial effect was driving the observed negative effect of diversity on violence, I ran additional regression analyses (results available upon request) replacing the diversity index with the percent African-American. For the purposes of this study, the percent African- American is defined as the percent of the total population who identified themselves as black or African-American, and non-Hispanic.[33] Although highly correlated with poverty (.70),

---

33 A variety of racial categorizations are possible using Census 2000 data. The non-Hispanic black measure used here also includes multi-racial individuals. Specifically, this measure includes all non-Hispanic and non-Asian persons who indicated they were Black or African-American.

Table 6.9 Negative Binomial Regression of Instrumental Violence on Immigration and Neighborhood Structural Factors, Alexandria 2000.

	Recent Immigrant			Salvadoran			Ethiopian			Honduran			Ghanian		
	(1)	(2)	(3)	(1)	(2)	(3)	(1)	(2)	(3)	(1)	(2)	(3)	(1)	(2)	(3)
Social Disorganization															
Poverty	0.06 **	--	0.06 *	0.06 **	--	0.06 *	0.06 **	--	0.06 *	0.06 **	--	0.06 *	0.06 **	--	0.06 **
Diversity	-1.67 **	--	-1.68 *	-1.67 **	--	-1.32	-1.67 **	--	-1.64 *	-1.67 **	--	-1.18	-1.67 **	--	-1.02
Residential Instability	0.08	--	0.09	0.08	--	0.10 *	0.08	--	0.08	0.08	--	0.10 *	0.08	--	0.10 *
Immigration	--	0.02	-0.01	--	0.05	0.03	--	-0.02	-0.02	--	0.09	0.06	--	0.02	-0.14
Control Variables															
Unemployment	0.16 **	0.17 **	0.17 **	0.16 **	0.11	0.12	0.16 **	0.18 *	0.16 **	0.16 **	0.12	0.12	0.16 **	0.19 *	0.13 *
Males Aged 18-24	0.01	0.01	0.08	0.01	0.00	-0.05	0.01	0.09	0.02	0.01	0.03	-0.04	0.01	0.08	0.03
Spatial Lag	--	--	0.10	--	--	0.09	--	--	0.10	--	--	0.14	--	--	0.11
Intercept	-6.96 ***	0.74 *	-7.60 ***	-6.96 ***	1.00 **	-7.32 ***	-6.96 ***	0.63 *	-7.50 ***	-6.96 ***	0.96 **	-7.63 ***	-6.96 ***	0.61 *	-7.73 ***
N[a]	(32)														

* p< .05, ** p< .01, *** p < .001
Note: Dependent variable is the average annual count of robberies between 1999-2001.
[a] Calculations are based on the same number of tracts are in each model

including both indicators in the models did not produce biased estimates, as none of the VIF values exceeded 4.0. Unlike the significant negative impact of the diversity index, the percent black did not have an independent effect on violence in any of the models, as might have been expected. Interestingly, introducing this alternative measure of racial composition did affect some of the results for immigration. For example, recent immigration was found to have a significant negative association with all three types of violence. Rather than a null effect, the presence of Salvadoran and Honduran immigrants had a significant positive influence on overall levels of violence. A direct positive relationship also emerged between the size of the foreign-born Honduran population and levels of expressive violence.

It is not entirely surprising that the positive impacts of immigration on violence are found among the Hispanic immigrant groups. As the descriptive findings discussed in Chapter 5 clearly indicated, of Alexandria's four largest ethnic groups, the Central American ethnics reside in the most structurally disadvantaged neighborhoods. This is particularly true for Honduran immigrants, who tend to live in areas with the lowest median household incomes, and the highest levels of poverty and unemployment, relative to the other groups. Although controlling for the percent African-American did change some of the observed relationships, the inclusion of this measure did not change the broader substantive interpretation of the impacts of immigration on violent criminal behavior in this city. The results using both measures of demographic composition show the salience of including ethnic-specific measures of immigration in order to understand more completely the full range of effects of immigration on violence.

Similarly, the results presented here do not support the argument that immigration is more likely to be associated with high levels instrumental violence. However, it is possible that this finding is a product of the somewhat narrow definition of instrumental crime used in this study. For example, it may be that levels of immigration are positively related to less serious forms of property crime that are not violent in nature (i.e., burglary, larceny). To the extent that such a process operates, it would not be identified in this study. Moreover, the limitations of available data prevent a closer examination of this question in the present study. These results nevertheless challenge the contention that the relationship between immigration and crime varies by type of offense.

A related topic that merits further attention here is the issue of immigrant generation. Although the multivariate models include controls for the presence of foreign-born ethnics, it is possible that the observed "immigration" effects are capturing the "ethnic" influence more generally.   Under conditions where native and foreign-born members of an ethnic group share neighborhoods, it may be difficult to isolate the unique impact of the size of the foreign-born population on observed levels of criminal violence.   To distinguish between the immigration and native effects on violence, I re-estimate regression models that include controls for both native- and foreign-born ethnic populations.   Before moving to the multivariate analyses, I will first describe the nativity characteristics of the primary ethnic populations in Alexandria.   For three of the largest immigrant groups, the ethnic population is overwhelmingly foreign-born, indicating that the share of native-born ethnics has only limited statistical influence. Specifically, over 85 percent of Hondurans, Ethiopians, and Ghanians in Alexandria were born outside of the US (91%, 87%, and 85%, respectively).   In absolute terms, this means that there were only 118 native-born Hondurans living in Alexandria in 2000, compared to 339 Ethiopians and 182 Ghanians.[34]   Further, such small overall numbers will make it difficult to obtain reliable regression estimates.

There are approximately 1,350 native-born Salvadorans living in Alexandria, which represents about 24% of the city's ethnic population. While there are sufficient numbers of individuals to estimate the effects of both groups, these variables are highly correlated (.87). Such a high correlation indicates that including both ethnic measures in the same regression model will produced biased estimates (see Land et al. 1990). Regression diagnostics also confirmed the presence of multicollinearity between these variables, as the VIF value was 7.7, nearly twice the conventional threshold for acceptability.   To no surprise, the results from multivariate analyses that include the native-born Salvadoran ethnic variable are consistent with those that employed the measure of immigration (results available upon request).   In both cases, the presence of Salvadorans is significantly related to levels of overall and expressive violence in the models that control for demographic composition using the percent African-American (instead of the diversity index).   Based on these findings, it is not possible to determine the extent to which positive impacts on violence can be attributed to immigration.

The finding that immigration has negative, or null, effects on violent crime is consistent with those reported in earlier studies

---

34 Ethnic-specific data taken from Census 2000 Summary File 4.

(Martinez and Lee 1998, 2000a; Lee et al. 2001; Lee 2003). In prior research, the null-effects of immigration are interpreted as running counter to the expectations of disorganization theory. As Lee et al. (2001: 571) argue, the non-findings do not support "either the popular stereotypes...or the expectations derived from sociological theories." However, it is important to keep in mind that these conclusions are drawn from analyses that do not consider the impact of immigration on neighborhood social structure. When the influence of immigration on social structure is considered, the results for Alexandria are supportive of the theoretical arguments claiming that immigration is associated with higher levels of economic disadvantage and racial/ethnic diversity. In other words, the initial multivariate findings are consistent with the perception of immigration as a social process that affects neighborhood social structure. This is especially apparent with regards to levels of economic deprivation. The multivariate findings show that, as disorganization theory predicts, immigration is indirectly linked to violence through poverty. Yet these results also illustrate the limitations in assuming homogeneity among the foreign-born population. As is clear in the findings for Alexandria, there are variations across immigrant ethnic groups in terms of both their impacts on neighborhood structural characteristics and violence.

Houston

Although there are similarities in the models predicting overall levels of neighborhood violence in Houston and Alexandria, there are also a number of differences in causal patterns observed between cities. First, we again see that neighborhood economic disadvantage is a strong predictor of violent criminal behavior. For each of the models presented in Table 6.10, neighborhood poverty rates have a significant positive impact on violence. Each of the other commonly used proxies for disorganization also is systematically related to levels of violent crime. Contrary to the findings for Alexandria, the racial/ethnic diversity of neighborhoods is positively associated with levels of violence in the Mexican, Vietnamese, and Chinese models. In the other two models, neighborhood racial/ethnic heterogeneity nearly reaches levels of statistical significance (p< .06 in each model). Alternatively, in the models for recent immigrants and Salvadorans we see that residential instability predicts higher levels of violence. In the remaining three models, the magnitude of the effect for instability falls just below the conventional threshold to be considered statistically significant (p< .06 in each model). As they relate to the indicators of social disorganization, the results for Houston are generally more consistent with the expectations of disorganization theory. This is indicated by the fact that each of the proxies for disorganization is positively associated with crime, and that each has a non-trivial impact on observed levels of violent criminal conduct. Even when the impact of diversity or residential instability is not statistically significant using conventional standards, it may be inappropriate to consider their impacts unimportant.

The results presented in Table 6.10 pertaining to the other control variables do not support the research hypotheses. While a positive relationship was expected, according to these results, violence in Houston is not influenced by either unemployment rates or the size of the young adult male population. The inability of these variables to predict criminal violence is unexpected given the fact that prior immigration research has found that community age-structure and involvement in the formal economy have independent effects on crime (see Lee et al. 2001; Lee 2003). A potential concern is that the null findings for the control variables are a product of high correlations among the independent variables, and particularly between unemployment and poverty. As mentioned previously, the model diagnostics do not indicate that multicollinearity is present in the models. Although not a product of multicollinearity, it is possible that the effect of unemployment is a being suppressed due to methodological limitations. Specifically, as Cantor and Land (1985) argue, in order to observe the overall impact of unemployment it is important to control for its influence on both the motivation and opportunity to engage in crime. However, such considerations could not be included here because they require the use of a longitudinal analytical framework. Nevertheless, based on the data used in this study neither of the controls contributes substantively to our understanding of the factors that predict violence in Houston.

Whereas it was unrelated to crime in Alexandria, the spatial lag variable has a strong relationship with violence in Houston. In Table 6.10 we observe that the spatial term has a positive influence on levels of violent criminal conduct in every model. Aside from poverty, the prevalence of crime in surrounding neighborhoods is the strongest predictor of a neighborhood's observed levels of violence. The spatial effect is also consistent across models, as indicated by the stability in the size of the regression coefficients. The finding of statistically significant spatial dependence is consistent with both the descriptive

Table 6.10 Negative Binomial Regression of Violent Crime on Immigration and Neighborhood Structural Factors, Houston 2000.

	Recent Immigrant			Mexican			Salvadoran			Vietnamese			Chinese		
	(1)	(2)	(3)	(1)	(2)	(3)	(1)	(2)	(3)	(1)	(2)	(3)	(1)	(2)	(3)
Social Disorganization															
Poverty	0.07 ***	--	0.04 ***	0.07 ***	--	0.04 ***	0.07 ***	--	0.04 ***	0.07 ***	--	0.04 ***	0.07 ***	--	0.04 ***
Diversity	0.23	--	0.71	0.23	--	0.90 *	0.23	--	0.77	0.23	--	0.92 *	0.23	--	0.78 *
Residential Instability	0.06	--	0.09 *	0.06	--	0.08	0.06	--	0.09 *	0.06	--	0.08	0.06	--	0.08
Immigration	--	0.04 ***	0.01	--	0.01	0.00	--	0.13 ***	0.03	--	0.05	0.00	--	0.11 *	0.01
Control Variables															
Unemployment	0.01	0.11 ***	0.00	0.01	0.09 ***	-0.01	0.01	0.10 ***	-0.01	0.01	0.10 ***	-0.01	0.01	0.10 ***	-0.01
Males Aged 18-24	-0.01	0.03	-0.05	-0.01	0.11 *	-0.02	-0.01	0.08 *	-0.03	-0.01	0.15 ***	-0.02	-0.01	0.15 ***	-0.02
Spatial Lag	--	--	0.10 ***	--	--	0.09 ***	--	--	0.09 ***	--	--	0.08 ***	--	--	0.09 ***
Intercept	-6.33 ***	2.09 ***	-10.90 ***	-6.33 ***	2.12 ***	-10.36 ***	-6.33 ***	2.12 ***	-10.64 ***	-6.33 ***	1.95 ***	-10.24 ***	-6.33 ***	1.87 ***	-10.63 ***
N^a	(516)														

* p< .05, ** p< .01, *** p < .001

Note: Dependent variable is the average annual count of homicides, aggravated assaults, and robberies between 1999-2001.

[a] Calculations are based on the same number of tracts are in each model

analyses and previous criminological research on immigration (see Lee et al. 2001; Lee and Martinez 2002; Lee 2003). This finding is supportive more generally of the notion that it is important for researchers to control statistically for spatial dependency when present (Baller et al. 2001; Anselin et al. 2001; Cohen and Tita 1999).

The initial multivariate analyses indicate that immigration does not directly impact overall levels of violent crime. In none of the fully-specified models is the size of a given immigrant population significantly related to violence. The results presented in Table 6.10 do show that the influence of immigration on violent crime operates through social structure, as social disorganization theory hypothesizes. For example, we observe substantial reductions in the size of the immigration coefficients between the second and third models for each of the five immigrant groups examined. In three instances (recent immigrant, Salvadoran, and Chinese models), the immigration effect is attenuated to non-significance by controlling for neighborhood social structural conditions. Due to the strong mediating influence of neighborhood social structure, these findings do not offer support to the claim that immigration may influence crime through two distinct causal pathways. Despite the lack of direct effects of immigration on violence, this should not be taken to suggest that the presence of each ethnic group has a similar effect on violence. Rather, the importance of including ethnic-specific measures of immigration is observed in their differential impacts on community social structure.

For the purposes of comparison, a brief discussion of the breakdown of violence into expressive and instrumental categories will precede the presentation of the offense-specific regression results. Official police department records contain information on nearly 64,000 violent offenses committed in Houston between 1999 and 2001 (compared to only 350 in Alexandria during the same period). Of the more than 21,000 violent crimes observed annually, a large portion is classified as expressive. Specifically, homicides and aggravated assaults comprise approximately 60% (12,414 annual average) of all violent crimes, while robberies account for the remaining 40% (8,800 annual average). While the distributions do not mirror the national averages (70% and 30%, respectively), the proportions in Houston are much closer to the national pattern than corresponding levels in Alexandria.

There are many similarities between the results from the analyses predicting expressive and instrumental crime and those for overall levels of violence (see Table 6.11 and Table 6.12). In both tables we

Table 6.11 Negative Binomial Regression of Expressive Violence on Immigration and Neighborhood Structural Factors, Houston 2000.

	Recent Immigrant			Mexican			Salvadoran			Vietnamese			Chinese		
	(1)	(2)	(3)	(1)	(2)	(3)	(1)	(2)	(3)	(1)	(2)	(3)	(1)	(2)	(3)
Social Disorganization															
Poverty	0.07 ***	--	0.05 ***	0.07 ***	--	0.05 ***	0.07 ***	--	0.05 ***	0.07 ***	--	0.05 ***	0.07 ***	--	0.05 ***
Diversity	0.16	--	0.78 *	0.16	--	0.88 *	0.16	--	0.77 *	0.16	--	0.85 *	0.16	--	0.84 *
Residential Instability	0.04	--	0.05	0.04	--	0.04	0.04	--	0.06	0.04	--	0.05	0.04	--	0.05
Immigration	--	0.03 ***	0.01	--	0.01	0.00	--	0.12 ***	0.03	--	0.04	0.00	--	0.07	0.00
Control Variables															
Unemployment	0.02	0.13 ***	0.02	0.02	0.12 ***	0.01	0.02	0.12 ***	0.01	0.02	0.12 ***	0.01	0.02	0.13 ***	0.01
Males Aged 18-24	-0.01	0.03	-0.03	-0.01	0.09 *	-0.01	-0.01	0.06	-0.03	-0.01	0.12 ***	-0.02	-0.01	0.12 ***	-0.02
Spatial Lag	--	--	0.09 ***	--	--	0.09 ***	--	--	0.10 ***	--	--	0.09 ***	--	--	0.11 ***
Intercept	-7.01 ***	1.45 ***	-9.64 ***	-7.01 ***	1.49 ***	-9.64 ***	-7.01 ***	1.48 ***	-9.74 ***	-7.01 ***	1.34 ***	-9.72 ***	-7.01 ***	1.30 ***	-10.10 ***

N[a]   (516)

* p< .05, ** p< .01, *** p < .001

Note: Dependent variable is the average annual count of homicides and aggravated assaults between 1999-2001.

[a] Calculations are based on the same number of tracts in each model

generally do not observe that the three indicators of social disorganization have consistent effects on the distinct forms of criminal violence. Poverty is the exception, as these results again show that economic deprivation has a strong positive influence on both categories of crime, net of other neighborhood characteristics. The results also show that the other indicators of disorganization, diversity and residential instability, are associated exclusively with only a single form of violence. For example, in Table 6.11 we see that for each of the five immigrant groups, the compositional diversity of neighborhoods is related to higher levels of expressive violence, while the impact of instability is null. The opposite is true for instrumental violence; residential instability is related to higher levels of criminal deviance and the impact of racial/ethnic heterogeneity is non-significant. Similar to the findings reported above, the results of these models do not resonate with the theoretical expectations, which hypothesize that crime is likely to result from the collective impact of these three structural factors.

Although diversity is related to violence as expected by disorganization theory, it is still instructive to check whether our substantive findings change when a more conventional measure of neighborhood racial composition is employed. To examine this question, the analytical models were run using percent African-American rather than the diversity index. In Table 6.13 we see that the size of the African-American population has a significant positive impact only on levels of expressive violence, an effect that emerges in the models for each ethnic group. This finding is somewhat different from the models described above, which find that the diversity index has a differential impact on the various forms of criminal violence. Unlike in prior analyses, the instability index has a more consistent impact on violence in the models that control for the presence of a single minority group. Although this appears to be a substantively important difference, recall that in the previous models the effect of residential stability approached levels of statistical significance (i.e., p<.06). Other than the small changes in the effect of residential instability, controlling for the presence of African-Americans does not change the observed effects of the other control variables. Of particular interest to this study, the use of this measure as an indicator of neighborhood demographic composition does not contribute to a more complete understanding of the relationship between immigration and violent crime.

Table 6.12 Negative Binomial Regression of Instrumental Violence on Immigration and Neighborhood Structural Factors, Houston 2000.

	Recent Immigrant			Mexican			Salvadoran			Vietnamese			Chinese		
	(1)	(2)	(3)	(1)	(2)	(3)	(1)	(2)	(3)	(1)	(2)	(3)	(1)	(2)	(3)
Social Disorganization															
Poverty	0.06 ***	--	0.04 ***	0.06 ***	--	0.03 ***	0.06 ***	--	0.04 ***	0.06 ***	--	0.04 ***	0.06 ***	--	0.04 ***
Diversity	0.39	--	0.23	0.39	--	0.60	0.39	--	0.47	0.39	--	0.79	0.39	--	0.49
Residential Instability	0.08 *	--	0.10 **	0.08 *	--	0.14 **	0.08 *	--	0.10 *	0.08 *	--	0.10 *	0.08 *	--	0.09 *
Immigration	--	0.05 ***	0.00	--	0.02 *	0.01	--	0.16 ***	0.01	--	0.05	-0.01	--	0.14 **	0.00
Control Variables															
Unemployment	-0.01	0.08 ***	-0.01	-0.01	0.05 ***	-0.01	-0.01	0.06 ***	-0.02	-0.01	0.06 ***	-0.02	-0.01	0.07 ***	-0.02
Males Aged 18-24	0.01	0.02	-0.02	0.01	0.13 **	-0.04	0.01	0.10 ***	-0.01	0.01	0.18 ***	-0.01	0.01	0.19 ***	0.00
Spatial Lag	--	--	0.30 ***	--	--	0.35 ***	--	--	0.32 ***	--	--	0.32 ***	--	--	0.29 ***
Intercept	-7.09 ***	1.34 ***	-12.56 ***	-7.09 ***	1.41 ***	-13.29 ***	-7.09 ***	1.38 ***	-12.88 ***	-7.09 ***	1.18 ***	-12.87 ***	-7.09 ***	1.06 ***	-12.40 ***
N^a	(516)														

* p< .05, ** p< .01, *** p < .001

Note: Dependent variable is the average annual count of robberies between 1999-2001.

[a] Calculations are based on the same number of tracts are in each model

Disaggregating violence into substantively distinct categories does not uncover any differences in the causal connections between neighborhood age structure or unemployment on crime. Again in both Table 6.11 and 6.12, we observe that neither diversity nor percent African-American is associated with levels of expressive or instrumental violence. The regression models also confirm the strength of the spatial autocorrelation observed in the maps. In the fully-specified models for each of the immigrant groups, the spatial term emerges as a significant predictor of violent criminal outcomes. Finally, we again see that neighborhood social structure mediates the effect of immigration on violence. In these results there is clear evidence indicating that the effect of immigration operates through social structure, as described by disorganization theory. A number of implications can be drawn based on this latter finding. First, because immigration is not directly related to violence in any of the final models, these results do not support the hypothesis that immigration influences crime through multiple causal channels. Second, the null effects of immigration also fail to substantiate the hypothesis that immigration has differential impacts on various forms of violence (see Hagan and Palloin 1999).

Although the weight of the evidence indicates that immigration is only indirectly related to violence in Houston, it is again important to identify whether these findings are capturing the unique effect of immigration. To address this question, separate analyses were conducted in an attempt to distinguish between the causal impacts on violence associated with broad generational differences across ethnic groups. Immigrants comprise more than three-quarters of the ethnic Salvadoran, Vietnamese, and Chinese populations in Houston (77.8%, 78.8%, and 79.3%, respectively). The distribution among Mexicans is noticeably different, as native-born ethnics represent a larger share of the total (51.5%). Bivariate correlations suggest that co-ethnics are likely to reside in the same neighborhoods. For each of the primary ethnic groups, there is a positive and statistically significant correlation between the percentage of immigrant and native-born individuals: Mexicans (.73), Salvadorans (.45), Vietnamese (.71), Chinese (.63). Although highly correlated, the diagnostic tests did not indicate that including both measures of ethnicity in the regression models would introduce multicollinearity.

The multivariate results show that the generational status of an ethnic group does impact violence differently (see Table 6.14). Table 6.14 presents the estimates for the fully-specified models which include

Table 6.13 Negative Binomial Regression of Violence on Immigration, Nativity, and Neighborhood Structural Factors, Houston 2000.

	Mexican			Salvadoran			Vietnamese			Chinese		
	(1)[b]	(2)[c]	(3)[d]	(1)[b]	(2)[c]	(3)[d]	(1)[b]	(2)[c]	(3)[d]	(1)[b]	(2)[c]	(3)[d]
Social Disorganization												
Poverty	0.03 **	0.04 *	0.03 *	0.04 ***	0.04 *	0.04 ***	0.04 ***	0.04 ***	0.04 ***	0.04 ***	0.04 ***	0.04 ***
% African-American	0.01	0.01 **	0.00	0.00	0.01 **	0.00	0.00	0.01 **	0.00	0.00	0.01 **	0.00
Residential Instability	0.13 **	0.10 *	0.16 ***	0.11 **	0.09 *	0.11 **	0.09 *	0.07	0.11 **	0.09 *	0.07	0.09 *
Immigration	0.01	0.02	0.01	-0.02	0.00	-0.01	0.03	0.03	0.01	0.04	0.03	0.01
Control Variables												
Unemployment	-0.01	0.00	-0.03	-0.02	0.00	-0.01	-0.02	-0.01	-0.02	-0.02	0.00	-0.01
Males Aged 18-24	-0.02	0.00	-0.02	-0.01	0.01	-0.01	0.02	0.02	0.01	0.02	0.02	0.01
Spatial Lag	0.08 ***	0.07 ***	0.35 ***	0.09 ***	0.09 ***	0.31 ***	0.08 ***	0.08 ***	0.31 ***	0.08 ***	0.09 ***	0.28 ***
Intercept	-9.50 ***	-8.80 ***	-12.90 ***	-10.08 ***	-9.22 ***	-12.56 ***	-9.60 ***	-9.16 ***	-12.35 ***	-10.05 ***	-9.48 ***	-12.10 ***
N[a]	(516)											

* p< .05, ** p< .01, *** p< .001

[a] Calculations are based on the same number of tracts are in each model

[b] Dependent variable is the average annual count of homicides, aggravated assaults, and robberies between 1999-2001.

[c] Dependent variable is the average annual count of homicides and aggravated assaults between 1999-2001.

[d] Dependent variable is the average annual count of robberies between 1999-2001.

Table 6.14 Negative Binomial Regression of Violence on Immigration, Nativity, and Neighborhood Structural Factors, Houston 2000.

	Mexican			Salvadoran			Vietnamese			Chinese		
	(1)[b]	(2)[c]	(3)[d]	(1)[b]	(2)[c]	(3)[d]	(1)[b]	(2)[c]	(3)[d]	(1)[b]	(2)[c]	(3)[d]
Social Disorganization												
Poverty	0.04 **	0.04 *	0.03 **	0.04 ***	0.04 ***	0.04 ***	0.04 ***	0.04 ***	0.03 ***	0.05 ***	0.05 ***	0.05 ***
Diversity	0.01 **	0.01 ***	0.01	0.01	0.01 **	0.00	0.00	0.01 *	0.00	0.00	0.01 **	0.00
Residential Instability	0.15 **	0.13 **	0.18 ***	0.17 **	0.15 **	0.16 ***	0.06	0.03	0.09	0.07	0.05	0.08
Ethnicity												
% Foreign-born	-0.01	-0.01	-0.01	0.02	0.02	-0.02	-0.04	-0.04	-0.04	-0.05	-0.09	-0.03
% Native	0.04 ***	0.05 *	0.03 ***	0.31 ***	0.31 ***	0.28 ***	0.23	0.24	0.20	0.40 **	0.48 **	0.24
Control Variables												
Unemployment	-0.03	-0.02	-0.03	-0.02	0.00	-0.01	-0.01	0.01	-0.01	-0.04	-0.02	-0.03
Males Aged 18-24	-0.02	-0.02	-0.03	-0.05	-0.04	-0.04	0.00	0.00	-0.01	0.02	0.03	0.01
Spatial Lag	0.04 **	0.03 *	0.25 ***	0.08 ***	0.08 ***	0.27 ***	0.07 ***	0.07 ***	0.27 ***	0.08 ***	0.09 ***	0.28 ***
Intercept	-8.09 ***	-7.75 ***	-11.26 ***	-9.72 ***	-9.10 ***	-11.80 ***	-9.08 ***	-8.77 ***	-11.66 ***	-10.16 ***	-9.65 ***	-12.00 ***
N[a]	(516)											

* p<.05, ** p<.01, *** p < .001

[a] Calculations are based on the same number of tracts are in each model

[b] Dependent variable is the average annual count of homicides, aggravated assaults, and robberies between 1999-2001.

[c] Dependent variable is the average annual count of homicides and aggravated assaults between 1999-2001.

[d] Dependent variable is the average annual count of robberies between 1999-2001.

measures of native-born ethnics for each of the primary groups. As we observe in this table, the percent foreign-born is not directly related to violence for any of the ethnic groups. However, we see that the presence of the native-born ethnics is consistently associated with high levels of violence. In eight of the twelve models, the presence of American-born ethnics has a positive and significant direct effect on all three forms of violence. Ethnic Vietnamese are the exception to this general pattern, as they are the only group where neither the native- or foreign-born populations are linked to observed levels of criminal violence. The apparent generational differences are consistent with the arguments advanced by immigration scholars who contend that across immigrant generations, those belonging to the second (and later) generations are likely to evaluate their opportunities according to American societal expectations (see Sampson and Bean 2006; Portes and Rumbaut 2001; Morenoff and Astor 2006). Further, perceiving that they have limited chances for conventional success, native-born ethnics may adopt "oppositional ideologies," which may include engaging in criminal activities (Portes and Rumbaut 2001, p. 60; see also Kao and Tienda 1995). Admittedly, the broad distinction between native-born and foreign-born ethnics is a very crude proxy for immigrant generation, and as such, these findings should be interpreted cautiously. Yet the consistency of these findings indicates that there are generational differences in the impacts of ethnicity on violence.

In one fundamental respect, the results for Houston are more supportive of the classical disorganization model than they are of prior immigration research. Specifically, unlike prior studies, these analyses do not find any evidence that immigration is directly associated with violence. The negative direct effect of immigration on crime that has consistently been documented in the research literature is not observed in Houston (Martinez 2002; Martinez and Lee 1998, 2000; Lee et al. 2001; Lee 2003) Instead, the results for Houston show that the influence of immigration operates primarily through its impact on neighborhood social structure. One possible explanation for the disparate findings may be due to the fact that the measures of violence used in this research are more broadly defined than those used in earlier studies, which focus primarily on lethal violence. It could be that there is something unique about the relationship between immigration and homicide that is not being picked up in the results presented above. To test whether the disparate findings are an artifact of how violence is operationalized, separate models were run using counts of homicide as the dependent variable. The results from this analysis (available upon request), however, do not show a direct negative impact of immigration on lethal violence for any of the foreign-born groups. Therefore, the inconsistencies between the results for Houston and prior research findings cannot be attributed to differences in the measurement of violence.[35]

Miami

A similar battery of regressions will now be discussed for the city of Miami. Because prior research has studied Miami extensively, in some ways, we have a more refined understanding of the immigrant/crime link in Miami than in any other American city (Martinez and Lee 1998, 2000b; Martinez 2002; Lee et al. 2000; 2001; Lee and Martinez 2002; Lee 2003; Nielsen et al. 2005). Previous scholarship has also included a number of other immigrant destination cities (i.e., San Diego, El Paso), however, the knowledge accumulated for these areas is not as complete as it is for Miami. Therefore, this research provides a unique opportunity to assess the conclusions drawn in prior studies, in light of the more extensive methodologies employed here. For that reason, when possible, the results from these models will be compared to findings reported in the existing research literature.

In the initial models for Miami, we again see that poverty has the strongest influence on overall levels of violence (see Table 6.15). For each of the ethnic groups, poverty is the only indicator of disorganization that is significantly related to levels of violent criminal behavior. This finding is consistent with both the pattern observed for the other two cities included in this study and previous criminological research more generally (Warner and Pierce 1993; Krivo and Peterson 1996; Sampson 1987; Lee et al. 2001). The null effect of residential instability on violence is another finding that is not entirely unexpected, given that it has not been shown to be an important predictor of lethal violence in Miami (Lee 2003; Lee et al. 2001). In Table 6.15 there is no evidence that overall levels of violent criminal behavior are influenced by neighborhood demographic composition, a finding at odds with theoretical expectations. The more general pattern observed in this table is that these results again do not support the claims by

---

35 Due to its low number of homicides, similar tests could not be run for Alexandria. Between 1999-2001, a total of 11 homicides were committed, a count too small to produce reliable estimates.

disorganization theory that the three primary structural factors will have unique influences on observed levels of criminal behavior.

Similar to the findings for Houston, neither the percent males aged 18-24 nor the levels of unemployment contribute significantly to the explanation of violent behavior in any of the fully-specified models. Interestingly, earlier studies have also shown that, net of other factors, labor force participation and neighborhood age structure are unrelated to homicide in Miami (see Lee 2003; Lee et al. 2001; Nielsen et al. 2005). As was the case in Houston, it is possible that the true effect of unemployment is being obscured by the cross-sectional research design employed in the current study (see Cantor and Land 1985). In Table 6.15, we observe a strong positive influence of the spatial term on local levels of violence, indicating that levels of violence vary directly as a product of the prevalence of crime in surrounding communities. In four of the five models the spatially lagged measure of violence has a positive impact on overall violence. The Cuban model is the exception to this general pattern, where observed levels of violent criminal conduct are not spatially dependent. It is not immediately clear why the spatial term is not significant only in Cuban model. A possible interpretation is that this null effect reflects an insular quality present in the more established Cuban ethnic communities, which provide a buffer against extra-local influences (Wilson and Portes 1980; Portes and Rumbaut 2001).

Unlike the findings for the previous two cities, the results for Miami show a much clearer pattern of association between immigration and violence. In four of the five models we see that immigration has a significant impact on observed levels of violence criminal behavior. Consistent with prior research, the results show generally that levels of neighborhood violence in Miami vary inversely with the size of the foreign-born population. The results in the first model, where we find that the presence of recently arrived immigrants is related to lower levels criminal violence, are the most comparable with previous studies. This negative association holds for the other Hispanic ethnic groups, as the negative direct effect of immigration is observed in the fully-specified models for Cubans, Nicaraguans, and Hondurans. Similar to the results for Alexandria, the significant effect of immigration emerges in the fully-specified models. This pattern is not consistent with the theoretical argument that social structural conditions will have a mediating influence on the relationship between immigration and violence. Instead, these findings offer support for the notion that immigration influences crime through both direct and

Table 6.15 Negative Binomial Regression of Violent Crime on Immigration and Neighborhood Structural Factors, Miami 2000.

	Recent Immigrant			Cuban			Nicaraguan			Honduran			Haitian		
	(1)	(2)	(3)	(1)	(2)	(3)	(1)	(2)	(3)	(1)	(2)	(3)	(1)	(2)	(3)
Social Disorganization															
Poverty	0.04 ***	--	0.03 **	0.04 ***	--	0.02 *	0.04 ***	--	0.03 **	0.04 ***	--	0.03 **	0.04 ***	--	0.03 *
Diversity	0.32	--	0.16	0.32	--	-0.34	0.32	--	-0.31	0.32	--	0.05	0.32	--	-0.13
Residential Instability	0.12	--	0.04	0.12	--	0.05	0.12	--	0.07	0.12	--	0.07	0.12	--	0.10
Immigration	--	-0.01	-0.02 **	--	-0.01 *	-0.02 **	--	-0.01	-0.02 *	--	-0.02	-0.04 *	--	0.01	0.00
Control Variables															
Unemployment	-0.01	0.05 **	-0.02	-0.01	0.05 **	0.00	-0.01	0.06 ***	-0.02	-0.01	0.06 ***	-0.01	-0.01	0.06 ***	-0.01
Males Aged 18-24	0.02	0.10	0.08	0.02	0.06	0.03	0.02	0.09	0.07	0.02	0.09	0.05	0.02	0.07	0.02
Spatial Lag	--	--	0.02 **	--	--	0.01	--	--	0.02 ***	--	--	0.02 **	--	--	0.02 **
Intercept	-5.13 ***	3.74 ***	-6.29 ***	-5.13 ***	3.93 ***	-4.93 ***	-5.13 ***	3.50 ***	-7.25 ***	-5.13 ***	3.45 ***	-7.61 ***	-5.13 ***	3.42 ***	-7.00 ***
N[a]	(76)														

* p< .05, ** p< .01, *** p < .001

Note: Dependent variable is the average annual count of homicides, aggravated assaults, and robberies between 1999-2001.

[a] Calculations are based on the same number of tracts are in each model

indirect causal processes. Yet in the first series of regressions for Miami it is also apparent that the causal connections are not identical across groups, as the size of the foreign-born Haitian population is unrelated to levels of violent crime. Disparities in the causal linkages between immigration and violence support the notion that it is important for criminologists to move beyond the use of overall measures of immigration in order to achieve a more refined understanding of the immigrant/crime link.

Before discussing the multivariate results that examine the differential impacts of immigration on expressive and instrumental violence, I will first give a broad overview of the relative frequency of each of these indicators of violence in Miami. During the three-year period for which these data were collected, information on nearly 23,000 violent crimes was collected from official Miami Police Department records. Of the average of more than 7,500 violent crimes committed each year, homicides and aggravated assaults comprise fifty-seven percent of the total (4,294 annual average), while the robberies account for the remaining forty-three percent (3,239 annual average). The proportions of expressive and instrumental violence in Miami are similar to the distributions observed in Houston, however, they are noticeably different from the national pattern.

In Tables 6.16 and 6.17 we observe a high degree of consistency between the models for expressive and instrumental crime and overall levels of violence. For example, among the proxies for social disorganization, poverty is the only factor consistently associated with high levels of both types of violence. In nine of the ten fully-specified models, a positive effect of poverty on levels of violent criminal behavior emerges, net of other controls (the exception is the Cuban model, Table 6.17). Conversely, neither the racial/ethnic composition of neighborhoods nor residential stability is found to have a significant influence on violence. Based on the findings for Miami, there is little support for the theoretical presupposition that together poverty, diversity, and residential instability are the key conditions associated with high levels of neighborhood violence. Rather, the analyses presented here confirm what has been reported in prior literature; namely, that the levels of economic deprivation are the strongest predictors of neighborhood violence in Miami (see Lee 2003; Lee et al. 2001).

Similar to the results for Alexandria, the unexpected findings with respect to diversity raise questions as to whether the heterogeneity index is masking an underlying influence of race. Borrowing again from the logic of Warner and Pierce (1993), separate analyses were conducted that include the percent African-American, rather than the more comprehensive indicator of neighborhood racial composition. Performing the additional analyses was complicated somewhat by the fact that the size of the African-American population is highly correlated with a number of the other independent variables. For example, while there are strong positive bivariate associations between percent black and structural indicators such as poverty (.62) and unemployment (.55), the size of the non-Hispanic black population is inversely related to the Hispanic immigrant ethnic groups; Cubans (-.78), Nicaraguans (-.58), and Hondurans (-.45). Other than the relationship with Cubans, percent African-American also had high correlations with the spatially-lagged crime measures (approximately .66 for each group). To limit the amount of shared "covariate space" among the independent variables, and to reduce the likelihood of committing the partialling fallacy, the spatially-lagged terms were not included in re-estimated models (see Land et al. 1990, p. 942).

Table 6.18 contains the results from the additional regression analyses. Focusing first on the effect of racial composition, we observe that percent African-American has a significant positive impact on levels of all three forms of criminal violence. This finding stands in stark contrast to the results discussed in the previous analyses for this city where the diversity index was not found to be associated with violence for any of the ethnic groups. Another pattern that is evident in this table is that the effect of poverty is not as consistent as in the prior analyses. Due to the high inter-correlation between poverty and percent African-American, it is possible that the discrepancies are owing to partial collinearity.[36] Nevertheless, these results generally show that by controlling for the presence of a single racial minority, the findings are more consistent with the expectations of disorganization theory. This is indicated by the fact that residential instability index emerged as a significant predictor of levels of violence. For each of the groups other than Cubans, we see evidence that each of the proxies of social disorganization have independent effects on violence.

For some of the ethnic groups, the direct effect of immigration on violence changes when controlling for percent African-American. This is particularly true in the Nicaraguan models where, net of other

---

36   In all cases the VIF values approached the threshold value of 4.0. The VIF values ranged from 3.5 to 3.8, nearly a full point higher than the values in previous analyses.

Table 6.16 Negative Binomial Regression of Expressive Violence on Immigration and Neighborhood Structural Factors, Miami 2000.

	Recent Immigrant			Cuban			Nicaraguan			Honduran			Haitian		
	(1)	(2)	(3)	(1)	(2)	(3)	(1)	(2)	(3)	(1)	(2)	(3)	(1)	(2)	(3)
Social Disorganization															
Poverty	0.05 ***	–	0.03 ***	0.05 ***	–	0.03 **	0.05 ***	–	0.03 ***	0.05 ***	–	0.03 ***	0.05 ***	–	0.03 **
Diversity	-0.08	–	-0.07	-0.08	–	-0.67	-0.08	–	-0.52	-0.08	–	-0.12	-0.08	–	-0.41
Residential Instability	0.12	–	0.04	0.12	–	0.04	0.12	–	0.08	0.12	–	0.07	0.12	–	0.12
Immigration	–	-0.02 *	-0.03 ***	–	-0.01 **	-0.02 ***	–	-0.01	-0.02 *	–	-0.02	-0.04 **	–	0.01	0.00
Control Variables															
Unemployment	-0.01	0.06 ***	-0.02	-0.01	0.06 ***	0.00	-0.01	0.07 ***	-0.01	-0.01	0.07 ***	-0.01	-0.01	0.07 ***	-0.01
Males Aged 18-24	0.02	0.08	0.09	0.02	0.03	0.02	0.02	0.06	0.06	0.02	0.07	0.05	0.02	0.04	0.01
Spatial Lag	–	–	0.02 ***	–	–	0.01	–	–	0.03 ***	–	–	0.04 ***	–	–	0.03 **
Intercept	-5.81 ***	3.10 ***	-6.56 ***	-5.81 ***	3.28 ***	-5.34 ***	-5.81 ***	2.82 ***	-7.53 ***	-5.81 ***	2.79 ***	-8.10 ***	-5.81 ***	2.77 ***	-7.52 ***
N[a]	(76)														

* $p < .05$, ** $p < .01$, *** $p < .001$

Note: Dependent variable is the average annual count of homicides and aggravated assaults between 1999-2001.

[a] Calculations are based on the same number of tracts are in each model

Table 6.17 Negative Binomial Regression of Instrumental Violence on Immigration and Neighborhood Structural Factors, Miami 2000.

	Recent Immigrant			Cuban			Nicaraguan			Honduran			Haitian		
	(1)	(2)	(3)	(1)	(2)	(3)	(1)	(2)	(3)	(1)	(2)	(3)	(1)	(2)	(3)
Social Disorganization															
Poverty	0.04 ***	–	0.02 *	0.04 ***	–	0.02	0.04 ***	–	0.03 *	0.04 ***	–	0.03 *	0.04 ***	–	0.03 *
Diversity	0.95	–	0.53	0.95	–	0.14	0.95	–	0.02	0.95	–	0.41	0.95	–	0.25
Residential Instability	0.09	–	0.03	0.09	–	0.04	0.09	–	0.05	0.09	–	0.06	0.09	–	0.08
Immigration	–	-0.01	-0.02 *	–	-0.01 **	-0.01 *	–	-0.02	-0.02 *	–	-0.02	-0.03	–	0.01	0.00
Control Variables															
Unemployment	-0.01	0.04 *	-0.02	-0.01	0.03	-0.01	-0.01	0.04 *	-0.03	-0.01	0.04 **	-0.02	-0.01	0.04 *	-0.02
Males Aged 18-24	0.05	0.12	0.09	0.05	0.09	0.05	0.05	0.12	0.09	0.05	0.12	0.07	0.05	0.10	0.05
Spatial Lag	–	–	0.04 ***	–	–	0.02	–	–	0.06 ***	–	–	0.05 *	–	–	0.05 *
Intercept	-6.01 ***	2.98 ***	-7.41 ***	-6.01 ***	3.21 ***	-6.15 ***	-6.01 ***	2.83 ***	-8.32 ***	-6.01 ***	2.76 ***	-8.47 ***	-6.01 ***	2.70 ***	-7.99 ***
N^a	(76)														

* $p<.05$, ** $p<.01$, *** $p<.001$

Note: Dependent variable is the average annual count of robberies between 1999-2001.

[a] Calculations are based on the same number of tracts are in each model

factors, the size of the foreign-born population is unrelated to levels of violence. Recall that in the previous tables, the presence of Nicaraguan immigrants was shown to have a significant negative impact on all three forms of violence. It should be noted that although they never reach the conventional standards to be considered statistically significant, the effect for Nicaraguans approaches levels of statistical significance in each of the models (p<.07 for each). Similarly, the size of the Honduran immigrant population is not directly associated with any of the three types of crime. Unlike the results for Nicaraguans, however, the observed relationships for Hondurans do not fall just outside of the range of statistical significance. In these analyses, the non-significant direct effect for Haitians is consistent with the results presented in previous tables. Although the picture changes a bit, using a specific measure of neighborhood racial composition contributes to a more complete understanding of the conditions associated with high levels of violence in Miami. More generally, the findings from these additional regressions show support for the notion that, contrary to the logic of disorganization theory, under certain conditions racial homogeneity may be associated with higher observed levels of crime (Warner and Pierce 1993).

Also consistent with prior research on Miami, these analyses fail to find an association between either unemployment or the percent of the population who are males between the ages of 18 and 24 and violence. As mentioned above, due to limitations in available data, the former relationship cannot be explored more thoroughly here (see Cantor and Land 1985). These results also illustrate that extra-local violence influences observed levels of both expressive and instrumental violence. In eight of the ten models, the spatial term has a significant positive effect on violence. Mirroring the results for overall violence, the Cuban models are the only ones in which the spatially lagged measure of violence does not have a meaningful impact on local crime. The null spatial effect in the Cuban models may be reflective of more developed informal observational and social control networks operating in these neighborhoods, or what Sampson and colleagues refer to as collective efficacy (see Sampson et al. 1997; Sampson and Raudenbush 1999; Morenoff et al. 2001).

With few exceptions, immigration is found to have a negative direct effect on both forms of violent crime. In Table 6.16, which includes the results from the analyses predicting interpersonal violence, we observe a direct inverse relationship of immigration on crime for each of the ethnic groups except Haitians. According to the Hagan and

Table 6.18 Negative Binomial Regression of Violence on Immigration, Nativity, and Neighborhood Structural Factors, Miami 2000.

	Cuban			Nicaraguan			Honduran			Haitian		
	(1)[b]	(2)[c]	(3)[d]	(1)[b]	(2)[c]	(3)[d]	(1)[b]	(2)[c]	(3)[d]	(1)[b]	(2)[c]	(3)[d]
Social Disorganization												
Poverty	0.02 *	0.03 *	0.02	0.02	0.02 *	0.02	0.02	0.02 **	0.01	0.02 *	0.03 **	0.01
% African-American	0.00	0.01 **	0.00	0.01 ***	0.01 ***	0.01 **	0.01 ***	0.02 ***	0.01 ***	0.01 ***	0.02 ***	0.01 ***
Residential Instability	0.06	0.05	0.06	0.15 *	0.13 *	0.15 *	0.16 **	0.13 *	0.19 **	0.13 *	0.10	0.17 *
Immigration	-0.01 *	-0.01 *	-0.02 **	0.00	-0.01	-0.01	0.04	0.03	0.04	-0.01	-0.01	0.00
Control Variables												
Unemployment	-0.01	-0.01	-0.01	-0.01	-0.01	-0.01	-0.01	-0.01	-0.01	-0.01	-0.01	-0.01
Males Aged 18-24	0.05	0.05	0.06	0.08	0.06	0.11	0.06	0.06	0.08	0.10	0.09 *	0.11
Intercept	-4.43 ***	-5.37 ***	-4.85 ***	-5.01 ***	-5.84 ***	-5.60 ***	-4.98 ***	-5.81 ***	-5.56 ***	-5.05 ***	-5.90 ***	-5.60 ***
N[a]	(76)											

* $p < .05$, ** $p < .01$, *** $p < .001$

[a] Calculations are based on the same number of tracts are in each model

[b] Dependent variable is the average annual count of homicides, aggravated assaults, and robberies between 1999-2001.

[c] Dependent variable is the average annual count of homicides and aggravated assaults between 1999-2001.

[d] Dependent variable is the average annual count of robberies between 1999-2001.

Palloni (1999) hypothesis, this negative association with levels of expressive violence is expected. However, there is no evidence that the size of the foreign-born population is associated with higher levels of property-based violence. Instead, the results presented in Table 6.17 show a negative effect of immigration for three of the five immigrant groups under investigation (recent immigrants, Cubans, and Nicaraguans), and a null effect in the remaining two (Hondurans and Haitians). This finding is consistent with the general lack of support this research has found for the Hagan and Palloni hypothesis.

To obtain a clearer understanding of the degree to which the observed negative influences are attributable to immigration, it is necessary to test once again for the differential impacts of nativity status on violence across ethnic groups. Because the ethnic populations in Miami are disproportionately foreign-born, it is likely that the causal effects are tied to immigration, rather than to ethnicity more generally. This is evidenced by the fact that nearly ninety percent of the Cuban, Nicaraguan, and Honduran populations in Miami were born abroad (86.9%, 87.1%, and 88.6%, respectively). Natives make up a larger share of the Haitian population, yet just over thirty percent (30.3%) of all ethnic Haitians living in Miami were born in the United States. Similar to the results for the other cities, correlation analyses also show positive and statistically significant associations between the native- and foreign-born ethnic populations: Cubans (.44), Nicaraguans (.65), Hondurans (.58), Haitians (.84). Except for Haitians, the associations between the two ethnic nativity groups are within acceptable limits for the purposes of multivariate analysis.

The results from the supplemental regression analyses are presented in Table 6.19. Haitians were not included these analyses because due to the high correlation, the independent effects of native-born and foreign-born ethnics could not be estimated. In this table we do observe that nativity has differential impacts on violence for each of the Hispanic ethnic populations. However, unlike the results for Houston, we do not see in Miami that the presence of US-born ethnics is related to high levels of violence. Rather, it is clear from this table that immigration, and not ethnicity, is driving the observed negative associations with levels of criminal violence. This is indicated by the fact that the native-born population is not significantly related to violence in any of the models presented in Table 6.19. By comparison, in six of the nine models, a significant negative relationship exists between the size of the foreign-born ethnic population and violence. Consistent with the results discussed above, the presence of Cuban and

Table 6.19 Negative Binomial Regression of Violence on Immigration, Nativity, and Neighborhood Structural Factors, Miami 2000.

	Cuban			Nicaraguan			Honduran		
	(1)[b]	(2)[c]	(3)[d]	(1)[b]	(2)[c]	(3)[d]	(1)[b]	(2)[c]	(3)[d]
Social Disorganization									
Poverty	0.02 *	0.03 **	0.02	0.03 **	0.03 ***	0.03 *	0.03 **	0.03 *	0.03 *
Diversity	-0.36	-0.70	0.12	-0.30	-0.52	0.04	0.06	-0.11	0.43
Residential Instability	0.04	0.04	0.03	0.08	0.08	0.06	0.07	0.08	0.06
Ethnicity									
% Foreign-born	-0.02 **	-0.02 ***	-0.01 *	-0.03	-0.03 *	-0.03 *	-0.04	-0.05 *	-0.04
% Native	0.00	0.00	0.00	0.00	0.00	0.00	0.04	0.05	0.06
Control Variables									
Unemployment	-0.01	-0.01	-0.01	-0.02	-0.01	-0.02	-0.01	0.00	-0.02
Males Aged 18-24	0.03	0.03	0.05	-0.30	-0.52	0.04	0.06	-0.11	0.43
Spatial Lag	0.01	0.01	0.02	0.02 **	0.03 *	0.05 **	0.02 **	0.04 ***	0.05 **
Intercept	-4.82 ***	-5.23 ***	-6.05 ***	-7.17 ***	-7.49 ***	-8.20 ***	-7.60 ***	-8.06 ***	-8.46 ***
N[a]	(76)								

* p< .05, ** p< .01, *** p < .001

[a] Calculations are based on the same number of tracts are in each model

[b] Dependent variable is the average annual count of homicides, aggravated assaults, and robberies between 1999-2001.

[c] Dependent variable is the average annual count of homicides and aggravated assaults between 1999-2001.

[d] Dependent variable is the average annual count of robberies between 1999-2001.

Nicaraguan immigrants have the most consistent negative impacts on violence. The results from these additional analyses provide strong empirical evidence that immigration has a unique influence on levels of violent crime in Miami.

In some ways, the results for Miami suggest that the processes through which immigration influences crime in Miami are different than in the other two cities. While the results for Houston were more supportive of the classical disorganization theory model, the results for Miami do not offer quantitative support for many of the central theoretical tenets. For example, other than poverty, we do not see that any of the neighborhood structural indicators related to either the overall or more refined measures of violence. Similarly, in each of the tables, there is no evidence of the mediating influence of social structure on the relationship between immigration and crime. Rather, a direct negative effect of immigration is observed in eleven of the fifteen fully-specified models. Contrary to the predictions of social disorganization theory, the direct effect of immigration emerges only in the fully-specified regression models. Finally, the consistency of the negative impact of immigration on violence is supportive of prior research findings.

Conclusion

The primary goal of this chapter was to examine the full range of effects of immigration on violence. At the beginning of this chapter, I described that the full range of effects is comprised of two conceptually distinct relationships; namely, the indirect and direct influences of immigration on observed levels of violent criminal behavior. Figure 6.1 is a graphical representation of the seven different causal relationships estimated in the multivariate analyses presented in this chapter (note that this is the same model first described in Chapter 1). The first regression results discussed in this chapter, represented by arrows 1 through 3 in the figure, examined disorganization theory's assertion that immigration is a social phenomenon that has negative consequences for the social structural composition of neighborhoods. This chapter concluded with the presentation of multivariate analyses that concentrated on the direct effects of immigration and other structural factors on violence (arrows 4 through 7 in the figure). In addition to testing whether immigration had a significant direct impact

Figure 6.1. Direct and Indirect effects of Immigration on Crime.

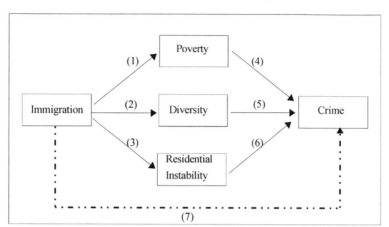

on violent crime, this research was also interested in understanding whether and to what degree social structure mediates the relationship between immigration and violent criminal deviance.

Because the results for each of the cities were discussed separately, it will be instructive to review the findings for all of the cities together. For ease of interpretation, a series of tables were created that summarize the findings from the multivariate models (see Tables 6.20 through 6.22). Note that the column numbers in these tables correspond to the regression arrows listed in Figure 6.1. The mathematical signs indicate whether a significant positive (or negative) association was observed in the fully-specified model for a given city, and the empty cells indicate that a given association was not statistically significant. In the final column, the one representing the direct effect of immigration on violence, an "A" designates that controlling for social structural factors attenuated the effect of immigration in the model for a specific ethnic group to non-significance. Taking the first row in Table 6.20 as an example, we see that recent immigration in Alexandria is positively associated with poverty and racial/ethnic diversity (Stage 1). We also observe that while the former predicts higher overall levels of violence, the latter is inversely related to violence (Stage 2). Additionally, the results also indicate that observed levels of violence in Alexandria are not linked to the presence of recent immigrants.

Table 6.20 Summary of Indirect and Direct Effects of Immigration on Overall Levels of Violence

	Stage 1			Stage 2			
	(1)	(2)	(3)	(4)	(5)	(6)	(7)
	Poverty	Diversity	Residential Instability	Poverty	Diversity	Residential Instability	Immigration
Alexandria							
Recent Immigrants	+	+		+	-		
Salvadoran	+	+		+	-	+	
Honduran	+			+	-	+	
Ethiopian		+		+			-
Ghanian	+	+		+		+	-
Houston							
Recent Immigrants	+	+	-	+		+	A
Mexican	+		-	+	+		
Salvadoan	+	+	-	+		+	A
Vietnamese		+		+	+		
Chinese	-	+		+	+		A
Miami							
Recent Immigrants	-		-	+			-
Cuban	-	-	-	+			-
Nicaraguan		-	-	+			-
Honduran			-	+			-
Haitian	+	+		+			

In more general terms, the multivariate analyses show inconsistent support for both theoretical expectations and prior research. Focusing first on the results from the State 1 regressions, we do not observe a clear pattern of association between immigration and the three structural conditions commonly used as proxies for social disorganization. Of the social structural characteristics associated with disorganization, immigration is most consistently associated with high levels of poverty and diversity. However, as the summary tables indicate, the positive impacts are not universal. More variation is observed for the influence of immigration on neighborhood levels of residential instability. A point that is clear from these tables is that there does not appear to be a single impact of immigration on neighborhood social structural characteristics, but rather the effects differ by city and across groups. This finding is of interest because

Table 6.21 Summary of Indirect and Direct Effects of Immigration on Expressive Violence

	Stage 1			Stage 2			
	(1)	(2)	(3)	(4)	(5)	(6)	(7)
	Poverty	Diversity	Residential Instability	Poverty	Diversity	Residential Instability	Immigration
Alexandria							
Recent Immigrants	+	+		+	-		
Salvadoran	+	+		+			
Honduran	+			+			
Ethiopian		+		+			-
Ghanian	+	+		+			
Houston							
Recent Immigrants	+	+	-	+	+		A
Mexican	+		-	+	+		
Salvadoan	+	+	-	+	+		A
Vietnamese		+		+	+		
Chinese	-	+		+	+		
Miami							
Recent Immigrants	-		-	+			-
Cuban	-	-	-	+			-
Nicaraguan	-	-	-	+			-
Honduran			-	+			-
Haitian	+	+		+			

it demonstrates the importance for criminologists to include more refined indicators of immigration in future research.

Due to the two-stage estimation procedure used in this study, the indirect effects of immigration cannot be calculated directly. Yet it stands to reason that an indirect relationship exists when a foreign-born population is associated with a given structural factor in Stage 1 (i.e., poverty), and that same indicator has a significant impact on violence in the Stage 2 models. Using this comparative method, there is some evidence of the presence of a positive indirect effect of immigration on violence, particularly through its influence on poverty. However, immigration is only associated with poverty in eight of the fifteen models, which suggests that it is not accurate to assume that immigration will necessarily lead to higher levels of violence due to its positive impact on poverty. There is also some indication that although

Table 6.22 Summary of Indirect and Direct Effects of Immigration on Instrumental Violence

	Stage 1			Stage 2			
	(1)	(2)	(3)	(4)	(5)	(6)	(7)
	Poverty	Diversity	Residential Instability	Poverty	Diversity	Residential Instability	Immigration
Alexandria							
Recent Immigrants	+	+		+	-		
Salvadoran	+	+		+		+	
Honduran	+			+		+	
Ethiopian		+		+	-		
Ghanian	+	+		+		+	
Houston							
Recent Immigrants	+	+	-	+		+	A
Mexican	+		-	+		+	A
Salvadoan	+	+	-	+		+	A
Vietnamese		+		+		+	
Chinese	-	+		+		+	A
Miami							
Recent Immigrants	-		-	+			-
Cuban	-	-	-	+			-
Nicaraguan		-	-	+			-
Honduran			-	+			
Haitian	+	+		+			

immigration is related to higher levels of diversity or residential instability, that these structural factors are not always associated with crime in the expected direction. Note the opposite signs for the effect of diversity in the Stage 1 and Stage 2 results for Alexandria, or the opposing signs for residential instability and levels of instrumental violence in Houston. Both examples suggest a negative indirect association exists between the presence of certain foreign-born ethnic populations and violence.

The strongest evidence that immigration influences crime indirectly, as disorganization theory describes, is found in Houston. First, in the Stage 1 results we see that immigration tends to be is positively associated with both high levels of poverty and racial/ethnic heterogeneity. In turn, in the Stage 2 models, we see that both poverty and diversity have independent positive effects on violence. Therefore, it stands to reason that because immigration in Houston is related to both of these structural factors, it is exerting an indirect influence on crime. Further, as we see in the final column in each table, the results indicate that the impact of immigration is operating largely through social structure, just as disorganization theory hypothesizes. Although the mediating influence of social structure is found in the models predicting all three forms of violent criminal behavior, the effect is most pronounced for overall and instrumental violence.

Similar to the analytical models used in prior research, the multivariate analyses presented in this chapter also examined the direct effect of immigration. These results did show partial support for prior research in that when a direct effect of immigration was observed, it predicted lower levels of violent criminal behavior. However, the direct effect of immigration emerged primarily in the analyses for Miami. Moreover, this negative relationship generally held for each of the three forms of violence. To a lesser extent, an inverse association was also observed in Alexandria. The presence of African ethnic groups in Alexandria was associated with lower levels of criminal violence. The inconsistent effects of immigration once again point out the limitations of assuming homogeneity among the foreign-born population. Further, the results underscore the importance of employing more refined measures of immigration, which capture the growing diversity among the foreign-born population in the United States.

CHAPTER 7

Conclusion:
Review and Directions for Future Research

The research contained in this book has addressed a number of issues pertaining to the issue of whether and to what degree immigration influences observed levels of criminal violence. A critique of previous criminological studies of immigration is that they have employed overall measures of immigration. Although the use of such broad measures has challenged many commonly held assumptions regarding the causal association between immigration and crime, it is argued here that such measures are not without limitation (Martinez 2002; Martinez and Lee 1998, 2000a; Lee 2003; Lee et al. 2001; Nielsen et al. 2005). In particular, this practice assumes homogeneity among the foreign-born population, a notion that does not square with the diversity of the current wave of immigration (Rumbaut et al. 2006; Alba et al. 1999; Alba and Nee 1997; Massey 1995; Kleniewski 1997). The descriptive analyses presented in Chapter 5 illustrate this underlying heterogeneity in the cities under investigation by comparing the structural conditions of the neighborhoods into which immigrant ethnic groups settle.

Building on the information gathered from the descriptive analyses, the multivariate analyses presented in Chapter 6 focus on a central tenet of the disorganization perspective, but one that has not been explored in existing studies. In particular, the regression analyses examined the full range of effects of immigration on violence. Rather than focusing solely on the direct impact of immigration, the models discussed in this chapter are sensitive to the possibility that immigration may influence crime through multiple causal mechanisms. Additionally, a goal of the research presented in Chapter 6 is to broaden current knowledge on the causal association between immigration and crime by analyzing a wider array of criminal outcomes than have been used in previous immigration/crime studies.

This final chapter includes a brief review of the findings presented in the previous analyses. The primary findings of this research will be highlighted, and the implications that they have for research on immigration and disorganization theory will also be discussed. Following a review of the contributions made by this research, a number of empirical and conceptual limitations of the current study will be addressed. In light of the recognized limitations, recommendations will be made regarding directions for future research on this topic. Finally, the concluding remarks in this chapter will center on the broader implications of this research; namely, the contributions that this study may make to ongoing academic and public policy discussions on the issue of immigration and crime.

Review of Research Findings

The research hypotheses tested in this study are concerned with obtaining a more complete understanding of three general aspects of the relationship between immigration and crime. First, this study examined the issue of national origin and whether it is important to introduce measures of ethnicity in the study of immigration and crime. Second, this research focused on the causal mechanisms through which immigration and crime are related. By modeling the full range of effects of immigration, the notion that immigration may have countervailing effects on observed levels of crime could be tested empirically. Finally, this study was concerned with the question of whether immigration has differential impacts on conceptually distinct domains of criminal violence. In the following discussion, the findings associated with each of these substantive areas will be reviewed.

The Importance of Ethnicity

The impact of ethnic-specific measures of immigration on violence is an aspect of the immigrant/crime relationship that criminologists have left largely unexplored. As mentioned above, previous research has typically employed broad indicators of immigration (i.e., percent foreign-born, percent recently arrived), measures that are not sensitive to important differences within the immigrant population (for exceptions see Reid et al. 2005; Martinez and Lee 1998; Nielsen et al. 2005; Lee and Martinez 2006). Although more refined measures of immigration are rarely used in the extant criminological literature, scholars have pointed out the need to include more substantively meaningful indicators. As a leading scholar in the field contends, advancement in our "understanding of the specific impacts of immigration on crime" requires scholars to consider the relationship of "each nationality separately" (Lee 2003, p. 132; see also Lee et al. 2001). Recognizing the importance of this suggestion, this study represents a systematic test for ethnic variations in the association with criminal deviance. Drawing from non-criminological research on immigration, studies which clearly document the heterogeneity among the foreign-born population, it was hypothesized that immigration would not have uniform impacts on neighborhood social structure, and by consequence, levels of violence. This expectation runs counter to the underlying logic of social disorganization theory.

Recall that the logic of the disorganization theory de-emphasizes the importance of "nativity and nationality composition[s]" of neighborhoods, focusing instead on the structural arrangements of communities (Shaw and McKay (1969 [1942]), p. 315). Implicit in this assertion is the belief that immigrants are likely to have similar transitional experiences upon arrival in the United States, and thus, they will be "sorted" into structurally equivalent neighborhoods. To test this assertion, the structural composition of the typical immigrant neighborhoods in each of the cities was compared. In the descriptive analysis, disparities in the social structural quality of neighborhoods were thought to reflect the differential residential attainment opportunities available to ethnic groups.

The tables presented in Chapter 5 offered little support for the disorganization theory's assumption that immigrants represent a generally homogeneous population. Instead, the results highlighted the diversity between groups, as there were pronounced differences in the social structural conditions of the neighborhoods into which members of various ethnicities settled. Not only were there differences in the overall demographic composition of immigrant neighborhoods, but disparities in the structural conditions associated with social disruption were also revealed. In each of the cities, there were wide disparities in the levels of neighborhood poverty experienced by the typical members of the primary foreign-born ethnic populations. There were also noticeable differences in the housing characteristics of the neighborhoods inhabited by different ethnic groups. In particular, these analyses illustrate that foreign-born ethnics tend to settle in areas with differing levels of housing vacancy and the presence of recent movers, both factors commonly used as indicators of residential instability. The value of these findings is that they underscore the need for criminologists to move beyond the conventional practice of treating immigrants as a homogeneous segment of the population.

Countervailing Effects of Immigration on Violence

The analyses of primary interest in this research were concerned with obtaining a more complete understanding of the causal mechanisms through which immigration is linked to levels of violent crime. To review, disorganization theory describes immigration as a social force that has a disruptive influence on the social structure of the neighborhoods into which immigrants settle. According to the logic of disorganization theory, immigration is thought to impact crime indirectly, operating largely through its influence on social structure. However, criminologists have not examined the degree to which immigration has a disorganizing effect on community social structure, as the theory describes. Because such tests are absent from extant literature, an important theoretical question remains unanswered. Reexamining the underlying theoretical arguments is not meant to discount the findings presented in prior research, as these studies have cast new light on a relationship that is still not well understood by criminologists or the larger public. Indeed, contemporary criminological research on immigration has consistently documented the unexpected negative direct association between immigration and violence, and particularly homicide (Martinez and Lee 2000a; Martinez 2002; Lee 2003; Lee and Martinez 2002; Hagan and Palloni 1998).

Although the expectations of immigration theory are at odds with those of the disorganization perspective, it is argued here that immigration theory provides a rationale for this observed negative direct relationship (Kao and Tienda 1995; Zhou and Bankston 1998; Portes 1996; Waters 1999; Portes and Rumbaut 2001; Tonry 1997). Yet the explanations for the direct effect do not comment on the indirect influences, leaving open the possibility that immigration may impact violence through two distinct causal pathways. An examination of this question was central to the analyses conducted in Chapter 6. The results from the multivariate analyses presented in this chapter showed mixed support for both prior research and the expectations of disorganization theory. Consistent with theoretical expectations, immigration was found to have significant impacts on neighborhood social structure. Specifically, the multivariate analyses indicate that a positive indirect effect of immigration operates most strongly through its influence on neighborhood poverty levels (see Tables 6.20-6.22).

To a lesser extent, immigration was also related to diversity, but the positive association between two indicators was primarily observed in Alexandria and Houston. A consistent, though unexpected, finding is that immigration was found to have a negative impact on levels of residential instability in a number of the fully-specified regression models. This particular result was observed in the models for Houston and Miami, and is admittedly counterintuitive. This finding proves difficult to interpret because it is inconsistent with both the logic of disorganization theory and prior immigration research. To speculate, it may be that the inverse association between immigration and residential instability reflects the fact that large shares of a given immigrant ethnic population have been in these cities for more than ten years. Data limitations prevented the disaggregation of the measures of immigration by ethnicity *and* recency of arrival. It is also possible that this result is capturing the fact that members of some ethnic groups may be less likely to move over time, due either to residential preference or the fact that they have limited residential alternatives (see Logan et al. 2002; Pedraza and Rumbaut 1996).

Although not universal, these results offer support for the theoretical notion that immigration impacts crime indirectly, operating through its influence on the social structural characteristics of neighborhoods. As anticipated, the use of analytical models that reflect more closely those described by classical disorganization theory present a more comprehensive picture of the relationship between immigration and crime. Yet an interesting finding is that the indirect associations are not always in the theoretically expected directions. Nevertheless, these analyses revealed an aspect of the relationship between immigration and crime that was described in the initial writings on disorganization, but which has been largely overlooked in prior research.

In terms of the direct effects, the most common finding is that immigration is not related to observed levels of criminal violence. The results for Miami were an exception to this overall trend, as the size of the foreign-born ethnic populations was consistently associated with low levels of violent crime. Moreover, the negative direct impact of immigration is consistent with much of the prior research that has analyzed data for this city (Martinez and Lee 2000b; Lee and Martinez 2002; Lee 2003; Lee et al. 2001). At least for Miami, the weight of the evidence suggests that immigration does impact violence through both direct and indirect causal channels. In the other two cities, such a clear pattern did not emerge. In only three of the additional thirty models run for Alexandria and Houston was a significant direct effect of immigration discovered. In all three instances, the direct effect was negative in direction and observed in Alexandria (Ethiopian and Ghanian models, Table 6.7; Ethiopian model, Table 6.8). In the broader picture, the null effects of ethnicity on violence mirror many of the findings reported in previous studies. Similarly, it is important to note that in no models was ethnicity positively associated with levels of neighborhood violence.

Differential Impacts of Immigration on Violence

The final avenue of inquiry was concerned with whether immigration has differential impacts on various forms of violent crime. This study is the first to examine this question directly, as prior research has concentrated primarily on the relationship between immigration and levels of lethal violence. The specific hypothesis pertaining to this question was drawn from the work of Hagan and Palloni (1999) who argue that due to limited occupational opportunities, many immigrants may engage in crime to ameliorate their difficult financial situations. According to the logic of the Hagan and Palloni argument, immigration is likely to be inversely associated with levels of interpersonal violence (expressive) and positively associated with property-based (instrumental) crime. To test this hypothesis, regression equations were estimated including these substantively distinct dimensions of violence as the dependent variables.

Decomposing violence into expressive and instrumental components did not reveal that immigration was more likely to be associated with specific forms of violence. In each of the cities included in this study, there was a high degree of consistency in the results from the models predicting overall, instrumental, and expressive violence. In no instance was immigration found to have opposite effects on instrumental and expressive violence. Instead, when a significant direct relationship between immigration and violence was observed, the effect was in a negative direction. This was particularly true in Miami, where the presence of immigrant groups was associated with low levels of both personal and property-based violence. Because this study focuses exclusively on the impact of immigration on violent crime, it is possible that the non-support for the Hagan and Palloni hypothesis is a product of how instrumental crime was operationalized. It may be that property-based violence is too similar in nature to other violent acts to detect the differential effects of immigration. Although the data were not available for the current study, it is possible that including non-violent offenses (i.e., theft, burglary) in the definition of instrumental crime would yield stronger support for the argument advanced by Hagan and Palloni (1999).

Additional Analyses

In the course of conducting this research, a number of additional analyses were performed to clarify key theoretical or empirical interpretations. First, to test whether the inconsistent impact of the diversity index was masking an underlying racial effect, the regression analyses were run using the percent African-American rather than the diversity index (see Tables 6.13 and 6.18). Contrary to theoretical expectations, these analyses demonstrated that racial/ethnic heterogeneity is not always associated with high levels of crime. Rather, consistent with prior research, the results showed that under certain conditions population *homogeneity* has a positive effect on violence (see Warner and Pierce 1993).

A second issue that could not be determined from the initial regression results was whether the impact of immigration could be distinguished from that of ethnicity more generally. To assess the extent to which there were disparate generational influences on crime, both the percent foreign-born and native-born of a given ethnic group were included as independent variables in the regression models. The results from these regression analyses showed that the effect of the foreign-born ethnic population was distinctly different from that of the native-born contingent (see Tables 6.14 and 6.19). While the size of the foreign-born ethnic populations was unrelated to violence in Houston, the presence of American-born ethnics had a significant positive impact on observed levels of violence. The opposite was true in Miami, where immigration was inversely associated with observed levels of criminal violence, and the influence of native-born ethnics was null. By teasing out the potentially confounding effects associated with immigrant generation, these findings suggest that the observed relationships between immigration and crime are capturing the unique effect of immigration on violence.

In summary, the results from the multivariate analyses offer both support for and challenges to social disorganization theory. Consistent with the propositions of the disorganization perspective, the regression results clearly document that immigration influences violence indirectly through its positive influence on poverty. In a majority of the models, we observed that immigration was positively associated with poverty, and that poverty predicted high levels of violence. The findings presented here also call into question a number of key assumptions upon which the theory is founded. First, the results demonstrate the importance of including ethnic-specific measures of immigration. Although the theory contends that it is unimportant for researchers to consider the nationality and/or ethnic composition of neighborhoods, this study found little empirical support for this particular argument. Further, these analyses have shown that the indirect effects of immigration are not always positive in direction, as evidenced by the fact that some foreign-born groups are inversely associated with residential instability. The inconsistent effect of diversity also suggests that racial/ethnic heterogeneity may no longer be a source of disorder, but rather it is racial isolation, and particularly the percent African-American, that is a stronger predictor of levels of criminal violence.

Limitations of the Research and Prospects for Future Study

As with any research project of this length, this study contains a number of limitations, which warrant further discussion. Because the analyses rely on secondary data sources, the limitations in this research center on data availability and measurement issues. A discussion of the limitations is not intended to call into question any of the conclusions drawn by this study, as the accuracy of the findings was a primary concern in the analytical strategy employed here. Rather, it is hoped that an awareness of some of the problems encountered will help to put the results into better perspective. It is in light of these shortcomings that avenues for future research on this topic can be identified.

One limitation of this research has to do with the two-stage estimation procedure. Although this method was appropriate for an examination of the relevant research questions, it does not allow for the overall, direct, and indirect effects of immigration to be quantified. While these effects could be inferred from the results, it was not possible to determine the actual strength of the observed relationships. For example, the effect sizes could not be gauged by multiplying the coefficients from the different stages, as is possible with the results from OLS regressions. However, OLS methods could not be used here due to the well-documented problems caused by using linear regression methods to predict tract-level crime rates (see Osgood 2000).

It should be noted that the general causal model upon which the multivariate analyses are based lends itself well to Structural Equation Modeling (SEM). The strength of SEM techniques is that they can determine solutions for entire systems of equations, such as the one presented in Figure 6.1. Before deciding on the two-stage approach, the possibility of using SEM was explored. This option was abandoned because, at the current time, SEM statistical software cannot estimate event-count regression equations. It seems likely that future advances in statistical software will accommodate mixed estimation procedures (linear and event-count components) within a single analytical system. Because of the specialized estimation requirements of this causal model, the application of SEM techniques will have to be reserved for later analyses.

The use of cross-sectional data makes it impossible to assess the extent to which immigration promotes the social disruption of communities, as disorganization theory predicts. The theory assumes a consistency in the structural composition of neighborhoods over time. The temporal argument underpinning disorganization theory is clear in Shaw and McKay's (1969 [1942]: 315) claim that crime becomes a fixed and "relatively constant" characteristic of particular neighborhoods. Further, disorganization theory is explicit in its assertion that high levels of neighborhood crime endure regardless of the nativity or nationality characteristics of their inhabitants. Current criminological scholarship on immigration also hypothesizes about the temporal effects of immigration on neighborhood social structure, though making an opposing claim (Lee 2003; Martinez and Lee 2002; Martinez 2006). In particular, the "Immigration Revitalization Perspective" promoted by Martinez and colleagues proposes that "immigration may encourage new forms of social organization that mediate disorganizing influences in inner city communities" (Lee 2003, p. 131; see also Martinez 2006). While the analyses presented here clearly show that immigration is associated with neighborhood social structure, what cannot be determined is whether immigration is associated with any changes (positive or negative) in neighborhood social structure over time.

Unfortunately the longitudinal crime data required to test these competing hypotheses are not widely available. Although efforts to gather longitudinal neighborhood-level crime data are currently underway, the task will be challenging and time-consuming. Collecting such data is challenging because gaining access to official police department records requires establishing relationships with department administrators and field officers. Further, the collection of these data takes considerable amounts of time because often the necessary information is not maintained in machine-readable formats, but rather has to be culled manually from paper copies of police reports (see Martinez 2002, p. xi-xiii). Data collection issues notwithstanding, future criminological studies of immigration will benefit greatly from the introduction of a longitudinal analytical framework.

One promising direction for future research, however, would be to apply a model similar to the one used by Schuerman and Kobrin (1986) in their study of "community careers in crime." Utilizing this method, a series of neighborhood types would be identified (i.e., emerging immigrant neighborhoods, enduring immigrant neighborhoods, declining immigrant neighborhoods) and monitored across decennial Census years. Tracking changes in the structural characteristics of these areas over time would provide insight into whether immigration is associated with "disorganizing" or "revitalizing" influences. Another direction for future longitudinal analyses could be to apply growth-curve modeling techniques to study the extent to which neighborhood violence trajectories vary as a produce of the arrival of immigrants over time (Nagin 2005; see also Griffiths and Chavez 2004).

Another limitation in the present study is that the data do not allow for a direct test of how neighborhood structural conditions influence the differential involvement in crime across immigrant generations. It is certainly true that much was learned from including the native-born ethnic population as separate predictor in the regression models. These results hinted at the fact that generational status is associated with differential impacts on observed levels of violence. Yet it should be noted that the measure used in this study represents only a crude proxy for generational status. While a broad distinction could be drawn between native- and foreign-born ethnics, data limitations prevented the construction of more-refined generational indicators. The Census does not make available tables that would allow the native-born ethnic populations to be further subdivided into second (native-born to foreign or mixed parents) or later (native-born to native parents) generational categories (see Portes and Rumbaut 2001). Therefore, it is not possible to determine if the differential impacts of generation are more strongly associated with the presence of second or third generation ethnics. Even creative uses of existing Census-based data sources will not resolve this problem (see Portes and Rumbaut 2001, p. 33). Perhaps a more viable alternative is for future research to focus on generational involvement in criminal behavior directly. This would require researchers to construct a data set that contains counts of crimes committed, or victimizations, as well as information on the ethnicity and nativity status of offenders (or victims). It may be possible to piece this information together from a number of disparate data sources; namely, interviews with police officers, official police department records, medical examiner records, marriage certificates, and/or birth certificates. Because of the complexity of such a data collection effort, ideally data would initially be collected for a rare criminal outcome, such as homicide. Despite the infrequent occurrence of homicide, compiling the necessary data would be a very labor-intensive and expensive undertaking. Such data would allow researchers to advance knowledge regarding an aspect of the relationship between immigration and crime that has yet to be fully explored (for exceptions see Sampson and Bean 2006; Morenoff and Astor 2006).

Another shortcoming of this research is one that is shared with tests of disorganization theory more generally. Specifically, this study does not include measures of the "intervening" neighborhood factors found to mediate the relationship between community social structure and crime (see Sampson and Groves 1989). Consistent with theoretical expectations, the work of Sampson and colleagues has shown strong support for the notion that neighborhood-level characteristics (i.e., collective efficacy, friendship networks) mediate much of the direct effect of structure on crime (Sampson and Groves 1989; Sampson and Raudenbush 1999; Sampson et al. 1997; Sampson et al. 2002). Further, the conclusions drawn in recent immigration scholarship imply that the observed negative/null effects of immigration may suggest that ethnic/immigrant neighborhoods are characterized by higher levels of collective efficacy. Although his analyses do not include measures of the community mechanisms, in *Latino Homicide,* Martinez (2002: 138) speculates that immigration "strengthen[s] communities," and by implication, results in lower levels of observed violence. Due to data limitations, measures of collective efficacy or cohesion could not be included in the present study. One potential resolution to this limitation would be to utilize the data collected by Sampson and colleagues as part of the Project on Human Development in Chicago Neighborhoods (PHDCN) to study immigration issues. Using PHDCN data it would possible to examine the degree to which levels of efficacy vary across immigrant and non-immigrant neighborhoods. Fortunately, research is currently underway to address some of these questions (see Sampson and Bean 2006; Morenoff and Astor 2006).

A final limitation of this research is its narrow geographical coverage. As mentioned previously, the size and/or diversity of the foreign-born populations in each of these cities made them well-suited for inclusion in this study. However, just as it is a concern with prior research, there are questions about the generalizablity of the findings based on such a small sample of cities. Although many of the large Hispanic ethnic groups are represented in this research, the same cannot be said for Asians. In this study, the impacts of immigration on crime were considered for only two foreign-born Asian groups. More generally, the under-representation of Asian ethnics in criminological research indicates that the immigrant/crime link is still not well understood for a large and growing segment of the immigrant population. Addressing this problem requires the gathering of tract-level crime data for cities with more diverse ethnic immigrant populations (i.e., New York, Los Angeles, Chicago). As mentioned above, the collection of such data is a difficult and time-consuming process. An initial step for future research may be to re-analyze data for San Diego, an immigrant destination city that has been included in prior studies (Lee 2003; Lee et al. 2001; Nielsen et al. 2005). Additional research using these data would be productive because they have not yet been used to examine the differential effects of ethnicity.

The disparate effects of immigration on the indicators of disorganization observed across cities also suggest the difficulty in drawing broad conclusions from these results. The findings presented in this study point out how the association between immigration and crime is influenced by the larger social context into which immigrants settle. Specifically, in their discussion of modes of immigrant incorporation, Portes and Rumbaut (2001) recognize the important role context plays in the formation of ethnic communities. Specifically, the modes of incorporation refer broadly to how warmly (or inhospitably) members of a given foreign-born ethnic group are received upon arrival in the United States. Although it is a multi-dimensional construct, the authors argue that "in particular, the governmental reception accorded to different nationalities conditions the chances for the rise of cohesive ethnic networks" (Portes and Rumbaut 2001, p. 65). Following this logic, it is possible that differences in immigration policy may help to explain variations in the relationship between immigration and violent crime both within and between geographical areas. Methodologically, multi-level modeling procedures could be employed to consider explicitly the effects of the social context into which immigrant ethnic groups are "nested." Although multi-level analytical approaches are scarce in the existing immigration literature, such analyses may play an important role in helping to explain geographic variations in the associations between immigration and violence.

Implications of Current Research

One of the primary goals of this study was to bring the topic of immigration back into the purview of contemporary criminological research. Given the exceptionally high rates of immigration the United States is currently experiencing, it is important now, just as it was nearly century ago, to examine the impacts that the arrival of these newcomers has on the receiving society. However, it is essential that contemporary immigration research is sensitive to the diverse cultural and demographic composition of the current wave of immigration, properties which distinguish the current era from previous periods of high immigration. In other words, a goal of this study was to better understand how immigration influences violence, but to do so from a contemporary sociological perspective. This research was successful in this regard, as it represents one of the initial criminological studies to examine systematically the differential impacts of ethnicity. Additionally, by including multiple indicators of violence, this research has contributed to a broader understanding of how immigration influences levels of criminal violence.

Another goal of this study was to conduct a test of disorganization theory that is more faithful to the classical theoretical writings. In particular, this research questioned whether the conclusion that disorganization theory is unable to account for the impact of immigration on crime was an artifact of the methodologies employed in prior studies. Based on the results of this study, it appears as though the findings that fail to find support for even "the basic tenets of the social disorganization perspective," are somewhat premature (Lee and

Martinez 2002, p. 363). Once the indirect effects are considered, it is clear that immigration does have a measurable impact on the social structural composition of the neighborhoods, and by consequence, violence. As noted, however, the indirect impacts are far from universal, nor are the influences always in the theoretically expected direction.

The indirect influence of immigration should not be overlooked, as in each of the cities immigration was clearly associated with neighborhood social structure. One of the most consistent findings was the positive indirect influence of immigration on crime through poverty. Indeed, the consistency of the indirect effect through poverty was documented in the results presented in Chapter 6. The challenges to the theory were observed in the less consistent indirect effects of immigration on the other proxies for social disorganization. Overall, because immigration was clearly found to influence the social structural characteristics of neighborhoods, these results show support for the general conceptual model offered by disorganization theory. Yet the substantive findings raise questions regarding the claims that immigration is a process that carries with it only negative consequences for the social structural composition of communities into which immigrants settle.

It is important to point out that while the findings discussed in this study do find broad support for disorganization theory's conceptual causal model, they also reveal the need for theoretical refinement. The calls for refinement are argued on different grounds than those commonly cited in prior research. Specifically, the findings in this study suggest that the primary limitation in the theory is not related to its underlying causal logic, but rather to its oversimplified conceptualization of the immigration process. Recall that the classical disorganization perspective explains crime using theoretical models first articulated by the urban ecological scholars of the Chicago School. Recent urban scholarship has shown the limitations of the straight-line assimilationist logic underpinning the ecological accounts of urban processes (see Alba et al. 1999; Logan et al. 2002; Alba and Nee 1997). Similarly, this study shows the inaccuracies of disorganization theory's assumption regarding the homogeneity of the immigrant population. Indeed, this research illustrates that there are important differences between immigrant groups, which manifest themselves in differential impacts on neighborhood social structure and violence.

Given the diversity of the current wave of immigration, perhaps we should be measured in our criticism of the classical disorganization theory's perception of immigration. It is possible that the theory was able to account accurately for the impacts associated with immigration during the specific historical period for which the authors were writing. In this sense, it may be unrealistic to expect the theory to explain accurately contemporary urban processes. The inability of the theory to account for the nuances of the relationship between immigration and crime may be an artifact of the increased "ecological differentiation" that has occurred since Shaw and McKay presented social disorganization theory (Bursik 1984, p. 402). In the recent past, criminologists have identified and empirically addressed a number of legitimate shortcomings in the classical disorganization perspective. It seems that the discussion of immigration can be added to that list. The theoretical critique offered by this study shares with those issued before by recognizing that, with modification, contemporary crime researchers can continue to benefit from the "power and generalizability" of the social disorganization perspective (Sampson and Groves 1989, p. 799).

As is clearly illustrated in this study, the relationship between immigration and crime is complex, and as such, not one that is easy to study empirically. I concur with Martinez and colleagues who argue that while academic interest in this topic is growing, much additional research is required before the intricacies of this relationship are well understood (Martinez and Lee 2000a; see also Martinez 2006). Nevertheless, the analyses conducted in this study have advanced our knowledge regarding the immigrant/crime link. Despite its methodological and conceptual limitations, this research contributes to a more complete understanding of the ways in which immigration influences levels of criminal violence. While it leaves many questions unresolved, this study represents a comprehensive and theoretically informed examination of the relationship between immigration and crime. It is hoped that the theoretical and conceptual advances made by this study will provide the foundation for continued research on this topic.

References

Alba, Richard D. and Victor Nee. 1997. "Rethinking Assimilation Theory for a New Era of Immigration." *International Migration Review* 31: 826-874.

Alba, Richard D., John R. Logan, Brian J. Stults, Gilbert Marzan, and Wenquan Zhang. 1999. "Immigrant groups in the suburbs: A reexamination of suburbanization and spatial assimilation," *American Sociological Review* 64: 446-60.

Anselin, Luc, Jacqueline Cohen, David Cook, Wilpen Gorr, and George Tita. 2000. "Spatial analyses of crime," In *Measurement and Analysis of Crime and Justice, Volume 4,* edited by D. Duffee. Criminal Justice 2000, National Institute of Justice.

Anselin, Luc. 2001. *SpaceStat, a software program for the analysis of spatial data, Version 1.91.* TerraSeer, Inc.

Baller, Robert D., Luc Anselin, Steven F. Messner, Glenn Deane, and Darnell F. Hawkins. 2001. "Structural Covariates of U.S. County Homicide Rates: Incorporating Spatial Effects." *Criminology* 39: 561-588.

Blau, Peter. 1977. *Inequality and Hetergeneity.* New York: Free Press.

Brimelow, Peter J. 1996. *Alien Nation.* New York: Random House Press.

Burgess, Ernest W. 1925. "The Growth of the City: An Introduction to a Research Project." In *Urban Patterns: Studies in Human Ecology,* edited by George A. Theodorson. University Park: Pennsylvania State University Press.

Bursik, Robert J. 1984. "Urban Dynamics and Ecological Studies of Delinquency." *Social Forces* 63: 393-413.

Bursik, Robert J. 1989. "Political Decision Making and Ecological Models of Delinquency: Conflict and Consequences." In *Theoretical Integration in the Study of Deviance and Crime: Problems and Perspectives,* edited by S. Messner, M. Krohn, and A. Liska. Albany: SUNY Press.

Bursik, Robert J. and Harold G. Grasmick. 1992. "Longitudinal Neighborhood Profiles in Delinquency: The Decomposition of Change." Journal of Quantitative Criminology 8: 247-63.

Butcher, Kristin F. and Anne Morrison Piehl. 1998a. "Recent Immigrants: Unexpected Implications for Crime and Incarceration." *Industrial and Labor Relations Review* 51: 654-679.

Butcher, Kristin F. and Anne Morrison Piehl. 1998b. "Cross-City Evidence on the Relationship Between Immigration and Crime." *Journal of Policy Analysis and Management* 17: 457- 493.

Cantor, David and Kenneth C. Land. 1985. "Unemployment and Crime Rates in the Post-World War II United States: A Theoretical and Empirical Analysis." *American Sociological Review* 50: 317-332.

Chiswick, Barry. 1979. "The Economic Progress of Immigrants: Some Apparently Universal Characteristics," in *Contemporary Economic Problems* edited by William Fellner. Washington, D.C.: American Enterprise Institute.

Cohen, Jacqueline and George Tita. 1999. "Diffusion in Homicide: Exploring a General Method for Detecting Spatial Diffusion Processes." *Journal of Quantitative Criminology* 15:451-493.

Cullen, Francis T. and Robert Agnew. 1999. *Criminological Theory: Past to Present.* Los Angeles: Roxbury Publishing.

Davis, James A., and Tom W. Smith. 1999. General Social Surveys, 1972-1998: [Cumulative File]. Chicago, IL: National Opinion Research Center [producer], 1999. Ann Arbor, MI: Inter-university Consortium for Political and Social Research [distributor], 1999.

Durkheim, Emile. 1951 [1897]. *Suicide: A Study in Sociology,* Free Press, New York.

Freeman, Richard B. 1996. "The Supply of Youths to Crime."In *Exploring the Underground Economy*, edited by Susan Pozo. Kalamzaoo, MI: W.E. Upjohn Institute for Employment Research

Gabor, T. and E. Gottheil. 1984. "Offender Characteristics and Spatial Mobility: An Empirical Study and Some Policy Implications." *Canadian Journal of Criminology* 26: 267-281.

Gonzales, Adolfo. 1996. *Historical Case Study: San Diego and Tijuana Border Region Relationship with the San Diego Police Department, 1957-1994.* Ann Arbor: UMI Dissertation Services.

Gottfredson, Michael and Travis Hirschi. 1986. "The True Value of Lamba Would Appear to be Zero: An Essay on Career Criminals, Selective Incapacitation, Cohort Studies, and Related Topics." *Criminology* 24: 213-234.

Griffiths, Elizabeth and Jorge Chavez. 2004. "Communities, Street Guns and Homicide Trajectories in Chicago, 1980-1995: Merging Methods for Examining Homicide Trends Across Space and Time." *Criminology* 42: 941-978.

Gurr, Ted R. 1989. "The History of Violent Crime in America." In *Violence in America, Volume 1* edited by Ted R. Gurr. Newbury Park: Sage Publications.

Hagan, John. 1994. *Crime and Disrepute.* Thousand Oaks: Pine Forge Press.

Hagan, John and Alberto Palloni. 1998. "Immigration and Crime in the United States." Pp. 367-387 in *The Immigration Debate* edited by James P. Smith and Barry Edmonston. Washington, DC: National Academy Press.

Hagan, John and Alberto Palloni. 1999. "Sociological Criminology and the Myth of Hispanic Immigration and Crime." *Social Problems* 46: 617-632.

Hawley, Amos. 1986. *Human Ecology: A Theoretical Essay.* Chicago: University of Chicago Press.

Heitgard, Janet L. and Robert J, Bursik. 1987. "Extracommunity Dynamics and the Ecology of Delinquency." *American Journal of Sociology* 92: 775-87.

Kao, Grace. 1995. "Asian Americans as Model Minorities? A Look at Their Academic Performance." *American Journal of Education* 103: 121-159.

Kao, Grace and Marta Tienda. 1995. "Optimism and Achievement: The Educational Performance of Immigrant Youth." *Social Science Quarterly* 76:1-19.

Kleniewski, Nancy. 1997. *Cities, Change, and Conflict: A Political Economy of Urban Life.* Belmont: Wadsworth Press.

Kornhauser, Ruth R. *Social Sources of Delinquency: An Appraisal of Analytic Models.* Chicago: University of Chicago Press.

Krivo, Lauren J. and Ruth D. Peterson. 1996. "Extremely Disadvantaged Neighborhoods and Urban Crime." *Social Forces* 75: 619-650.

LaFree, Gary, Robert J. Bursik, Sr., James Short, and Ralph B. Taylor. 2000. "The Changing Nature of Crime in America." edited by G. LaFree and R. Bursik. Washington, D.C.: National Institute of Justice.

Lamm, Richard D. and Gary Imhoff. 1985. *The Immigration Time Bomb: The Fragmenting of America.* New York: Truman Talley Press.

Land, Kenneth, Patricia L. McCall, and Lawrence E. Cohen. 1990. "Structural Covariates and Homicide Rates: Are There any Invariances Across Time and Space?" American Journal of Sociology 95: 922-963.

Lane, Roger. 1989. "On the Social Meaning of Homicide Trends in America." In *Violence in America, Volume 1* edited by Ted R. Gurr. Newbury Park: Sage Publications.

Lee, Matthew R. 2000. "Community Cohesion and Violent Predatory Victimization: A Theoretical Extension and Cross-National Test of Opportunity Theory." *Social Forces* 79: 683-706.

Lee, Matthew T. 2003. *Crime on the Border: Immigration and Homicide in Urban Communities.* New York: LFB Scholarly Publishing.

Lee, Matthew T. and Ramiro Martinez, Jr. 2002. "Social Disorganization Revisited: Mapping the Recent Immigration and Black Homicide Relationship in Northern Miami." *Sociological Focus* 35: 365-382.

Lee, Matthew T. and Ramiro Martinez, Jr. 2006. "Immigration and Asian Homicide Patterns in Urban and Suburban San Diego" In *Immigration and Crime: Race, Ethnicity, and Violence* edited by Ramiro Martinez, Jr. and Abel Valenzuela, Jr. New York: New York University Press.

Lee, Matthew T., Ramiro Martinez, Jr., and Fernando Rodriguez. 2000. "Contrasting Latinos in Homicide Research: The Victim and Offender Relationship in El Paso and Miami." *Social Science Quarterly* 14: 375-388.

Lee, Matthew T., Ramiro Martinez, Jr., and Richard Rosenfeld. 2001. "Does Immigration Increase Homicide? Negative Evidence From Three Border Cities." *The Sociological Quarterly* 42: 559-580.

Liao, Tim Futing. 1994. Interpreting Probability Models: Logit, Probit, and Other Generalized Linear Models. Thousand Oaks: Sage.

Liska, Allen E. and Paul E. Bellair.1995. "Violent-Crime Rates and Racial Composition: Convergence over Time." *American Journal of Sociology* 101: 578-610.

Liska, Allen E., John R. Logan, and Paul E. Bellair. 1998. "Race and Violent Crime in the Suburbs." *American Sociological Review* 63: 27-38.

Logan, John R. 2002. "Separate and Unequal: The Neighborhood Gap for Blacks and Hispanics in Metropolitan America." http://mumford1.dyndns.org/cen2000/SepUneq/SUReport/SU RepPage1.htm

Logan, John R., Richard Alba and Wenquan Zhang. 2002. "Immigrant Enclaves and Ethnic Communities in New York and Los Angeles. *American Sociological Review* 67: 299-322.

Lu, Younmei. 2003. "Getting Away With the Stolen Vehicle: An Investigation of Journey-After-Crime." *The Professional Geographer* 55: 422-433.

Martinez, Ramiro, Jr. 1996. "Latinos and Lethal Violence: The Impact of Poverty and Inequality." *Social Problems* 43:131-145.

Martinez, Ramiro, Jr. 2000. "Immigration and Urban Violence: The Link Between Immigrant Latinos and Types of Homicide." *Social Science Quarterly* 81: 363-374.

Martinez, Ramiro, Jr. 2002. *Latino Homicide: Immigration, Violence, and Community.* New York: Routledge Press.

Martinez, Ramiro, Jr. and Matthew T. Lee. 1998. "Immigration and the Ethnic Distribution of Homicide." *Homicide Studies* 2: 291-304.

Martinez, Ramiro, Jr. and Matthew T. Lee. 2000a. "On Immigration and Crime." In *Criminal Justice 2000: The Changing Nature of Crime, Volume I* edited by G. LaFree and R. Bursik. Washington, D.C.: National Institute of Justice.

Martinez, Ramiro, Jr. and Matthew T. Lee. 2000b. "Comparing the Context of Immigrant Homicides in Miami: Haitians, Jamaicans, and Mariels." *International Migration Review* 34: 793-811.

Massey, Douglass S. 1995. "Getting Away with Murder: Segregation and Violent Crime in America." *University of Pennsylvania Law Review* 143: 1203-1232.

Massey, Douglas S. and Nancy A. Denton. 1993. *American Apartheid: Segregation and the Making of the Underclass.* Cambridge: Harvard University Press.

Maume, Michael O. and Matthew R. Lee. 2003. "Social Institutions and Violence: A Sub-National Test of Institutional Anomie Theory." *Criminology* 41: 1137-1172.

McDonald, William F. 1997. "Crime and Illegal Immigration." National Institute of Justice Journal 232:2-10.

McIver, John P. 1981. "Criminal Mobility: A Review of Empirical Studies." in *Crime Spillover*, edited by S. Hakim and G. F. Rengert. Newbury Park: Sage Publications.

Miethe, Terance D. and David McDowell. 1993. "Contextual Effects in Models of Criminal Victimization." *Social Forces* 71:741-759.

Model, Suzanne. 1995. "West Indian Prosperity: Fact or Fiction?" *Social Problems* 42:535-553.

Morenoff, Jeffrey D. and Avraham Astor. 2006. "Immigrant Assimilation and Crime: Generational Differences in Youth Violence in Chicago." In *Immigration and Crime: Race, Ethnicity, and Violence* edited by Ramiro Martinez, Jr. and Abel Valenzuela, Jr. New York: New York University Press.

Morenoff, Jeffrey D. and Robert J. Sampson. 1997. "Violent Crime and The Spatial Dynamics of Neighborhood Transition: Chicago, 1970-1990." *Social Forces* 76: 31-64.

Morenoff, Jeffrey D., Robert J. Sampson, and Stephen W. Raudenbush. 2001. "Neighborhood Inequality, Collective Efficacy, and the Spatial Dynamics of Urban Violence." *Criminology* 39: 517-560.

Murray, Alan T., Ingrid McGuffog, John S. Western, and Patrick Mullins. 2001. "Exploratory Spatial Data Analysis Techniques for Examining Urban Crime." *British Journal of Criminology* 41:309-329.

Nagin, Daniel S. 2005. *Group-Based Modeling of Development.* Cambridge: Harvard University Press.

Nielsen, Amie L., Ramiro Martinez, Jr., and Matthew T. Lee. 2005. "Alcohol, Ethnicity, and Violence: The Role of Alcohol Availability and Other Community Factors for Latino and

Black Non-Lethal Violence." *The Sociological Quarterly* 46: 479-502.

Ogbu, John. 1991. *Minority Status and Schooling.* New York: Garland Press.

Osgood, D. Wayne. 2000. "Poisson-Based Regression Analysis of Aggregate Crime Rates." *Journal of Quantitative Criminology* 16: 21-43.

Ousey, Graham. 1999. "Homicide Structural Factors, and the Racial Invariance Assumption." *Criminology* 37:405-426.

Park, Robert E. 1936. "Human Ecology." *American Journal of Sociology* 42(1) 1-15.

Park, Robert E. and Ernest W. Burgess. 1967 [1925]. *The City.* Chicago: University of Chicago Press.

Parker, Karen F. and Patricia L. McCall. 1999. "Structural Conditions and Racial Homicide Patterns: A Look at the Multiple Disadvantages in Urban Areas." *Criminology* 37: 447-477.

Paulsen, Derek J. and Matthew B. Robinson. 2004. *Spatial Aspects of Crime: Theory and Practice.* Boston: Allyn and Bacon.

Pedraza, Silvia and Ruben G. Rumabut. 1996. *Origins and Destinies: Immigration, Race, and Ethnicity in America.* Belmont: Wadsworth Press

Perlmann, Joel and Roger Waldinger. 1997. "Second Generation Decline? Children of Immigrants, Past and Present: A Reconsideration." *International Migration Review* 31: 893-922.

Peterson, Ruth and Lauren J. Krivo. 1993. "Racial Segregation and Black Urban Homicide." *Social Forces* 71:1001-1026.

Portes, Alejandro. 1996. *The New Second Generation.* New York: Russell Sage Foundation.

Portes, Alejandro and Dag MacLeod. 1996. "Educational Progress of Children of Immigrants: The Roles of Class, Ethnicity, and School Context." *Sociology of Education* 69: 255-275.

Portes, Alejandro and Min Zhou. 1993. "The New Second Generation: Segmented Assimilation and Its Variants." *Annals of the American Academy of Political and Social Science* 530: 74-96.

Portes, Alejandro and Min Zhou. 1994. "Should Immigrants Assimilate?" *Public Interest* 116: 18-33.

Portes, Alejandro and Ruben G. Rumbaut. 2001. *Legacies: The Story of the Immigrant Second Generation.* Berkeley: University of California Press.

Reid, Lesley Williams, Harald E. Weiss, Robert M. Adelman, and Charles Jarett. 2005. "The Immigration-Crime Relationship: Evidence Across US Metropolitan Areas." *Social Science Research* 34: 757-780.

Reppetto, T. A. 1976. "Crime Prevention and the Displacement Phenomenon." *Crime and Delinquency* 22: 168-169.

Rhodes, W. M. and C. Conly. 1981. "Crime and Mobility: An Empirical Study." In *Environmental Criminology*, edited by P.J. Brantingham and P.L. Brantingham. Beverly Hills: Sage.

Rossmo, D. Kim. 2000. *Geographic Profiling*. New York: CRC Press.

Roundtree, Pamela Wilcox, Kenneth C. Land, and Terance D. Miethe. 1994. "Macro-Micro Integration in the Study of Victimization: A Hierarchical Logistic Model Analysis Across Seattle Neighborhoods." *Criminology* 32: 387-414.

Ruggles Steven, Matthew Sobek, Trent Alexander, Catherine A. Fitch, Ronald Goeken, Patricia Kelly Hall, Miriam King, and Chad Ronnander. *Integrated Public Use Microdata Series: Version 3.0* [Machine-readable database]. Minneapolis, MN: Minnesota Population Center [producer and distributor], 2004. http://www.ipums.org

Rumbaut, Ruben G. 1997. "Assimilation and Its Discontents: Between Rhetoric and Reality." *International Migration Review* 31: 923-960.

Rumbaut, Ruben G., Roberto G. Gonzales, Golnaz Komaie, Charlie V. Morgan, and Rosauro Tafoya-Estrada. 2006. "Immigration and Incarceration: Patterns and Predictors of Imprisonment Among First- and Second-Generation Young Adults." In *Immigration and Crime: Race, Ethnicity, and Violence* edited by Ramiro Martinez, Jr. and Abel Valenzuela, Jr. New York: New York University Press.

Sampson, Robert J. 1985. "Neighborhood and Crime: The Structural Determinants of Personal Victimization." *Journal of Research in Crime and Delinquency* 22: 7-40.

Sampson, Robert J. 1987. "Urban Black Violence: The Effect of male Joblessness and Family Disruption." *American Journal of Sociology* 93:348-382.

Sampson, Robert J. and Janet L. Lauritsen. 1997. "Racial and Ethnic Disparities in Crime and Criminal Justice in the United States." Pp. 311-374 in *Ethnicity, Crime, and Immigration: Comparative and Cross-National Perspectives*, edited by

Michael Tonry. Volume 21 of *Crime and Justice* Chicago: University of Chicago Press.

Sampson, Robert J. and Lydia Bean. 2006. "Cultural Mechanisms and Killing Fields: A Revised Theory of Community-Level Racial Inequality" in *The Many Colors of Crime: Inequalities of Race, Ethnicity and Crime in America*, edited by Ruth Peterson, Lauren Krivo and John Hagan. New York: New York University Press.

Sampson, Robert J. and Stephan W. Raudenbush. 1999. "Systematic Social Observation of Public Spaces: A New Look at Disorder in Urban Neighborhoods." *American Journal of Sociology* 105: 603-651.

Sampson, Robert J. and W. Byron Groves. 1989. "Community Structure and Crime: Testing Social-Disorganization Theory." *American Journal of Sociology* 94: 774-802.

Sampson, Robert J., Jeffrey D. Morenoff, and Thomas Gannon-Rowley. 2002. "Assessing 'Neighborhood Effects': Social Processes and New Directions in Research." *Annual Review of Sociology* 28: 443-478.

Sampson, Robert J., Steven W. Raudenbush and Felton Earls. 1997. "Neighborhoods and Violent Crime: Testing Social Disorganization Theory." *Science* 277: 918-924.

Sanderson, J. P. 1856. *Republican Landmarks: The Views and Opinions of American Statesmen on Foreign Immigration, Being a Collection of Statistics of Population, Crime, Pauperism, Etc.* Philadelphia: J. B. Lippincott Press.

Scalia, John. 1996. *Noncitizens in the Federal Criminal Criminal Justice System, 1984-1994.* Washington, DC: Bureau of Justice Statistics.

Schuerman, Leo and Soloman Kobrin. 1986. "Community Careers in Crime" Pp. 67-100 in *Communities and Crime* edited by Albert J. Reiss and Michael Tonry. Chicago: University of Chicago Press.

Shaw, Clifford R. and Henry D. McKay.1969 [1942]. *Juvenile Delinquency and Urban Areas.* Chicago: University of Chicago Press.

Shihadeh, Edward S. and Nicole Flynn. 1996. "Segregation and Crime: The Effect of Black Social Isolation on the Rates of Black Urban Violence." *Social Forces* 74: 1325-1352.

Short, James F. 1997. *Poverty, Ethnicity, and Violent Crime.* Boulder: Westview Press.

Thrasher, Frederich. 1963. *The Gang: A Study of 1313 gangs in Chicago.* Chicago: University of Chicago Press.

Thomas, William I. and Florian Znaniecki. 1920. *The Polish Peasant in Europe and America: Volume IV, Disorganization and Reorganization in Poland.* Boston: Gorham Press.

Tienda, Marta and Leif Jenson. 1988. "Nativity Differentials in Public Assistance Receipt: A Research Note." *Sociological Inquiry* 58: 306-321.

Tolnay, Stewart E., Glenn Deane, and E. M. Beck. 1996. "Vicarious Violence: Spatial Effects on Southern Lynchings, 1890-1919." American Journal of Sociology 102:788-815.

Tonry, Michael. 1997. "Ethnicity, Crime, and Immigration." Pp. 1-29 in *Ethnicity, Crime, and Immigration: Comparative and Cross-National Perspectives* edited by Michael Tonry. Chicago: University of Chicago Press.

U.S. Commission on Immigration Reform. 1994. *US Immigration Policy: Restoring Credibility.* Washington, D.C.: U.S. Commission on Immigration Reform.

U.S. Dept. of Commerce, Bureau of the Census. Census of Population and Housing, 2000 [United States]: Summary File 1 [Computer file]. 2nd ICPSR ed. Washington, DC: U.S. Dept. of Commerce, Bureau of the Census [producer], 2002. Ann Arbor, MI: Inter-university Consortium for Political and Social Research [distributor], 2002.

U.S. Dept. of Commerce, Bureau of the Census. Census of Population and Housing, 2000 [United States]: Summary File 3 [Computer file]. 2nd ICPSR ed. Washington, DC: U.S. Dept. of Commerce, Bureau of the Census [producer], 2004. Ann Arbor, MI: Inter-university Consortium for Political and Social Research [distributor], 2004.

U.S. Dept. of Commerce, Bureau of the Census. Census of Population and Housing, 2000 [United States]: Summary File 4 [Computer file]. ICPSR release. Washington, DC: U.S. Dept. of Commerce, Bureau of the Census [producer], 2003. Ann Arbor, MI: Inter-university Consortium for Political and Social Research [distributor], 2004.

Warner, Barbara D. and Glenn L. Pierce. 1993. "Reexamining Social Disorganization Using Calls to Police as a Measure of Crime." *Criminology* 31: 493-517.

Warner, Barbara D. and Pamela Wilcox Roundtree. 1997. "Local Social Ties in a Community and Crime Model: Questioning the Systematic Nature of Informal Social Control." *Social Problems* 44:520-536.

Waters, Mary C. 1999. *Black Identities: West Indian Immigrant Dreams and American Realities.* Cambridge: Harvard University Press.

Whyte, William F. 1955. *Street Corner Society: The Social Structure of an Italian Slum.* Chicago: University of Chicago Press.

Wickersham Commission. 1931. *National Commission on Law Observance and Enforcement: Crime and the Foreign Born.* Washington, D.C.: U.S. Government Printing Office.

Wiles, Paul and Andrew Costello. 2000. "The Road to Nowhere: The Evidence for Traveling Criminals." Home Office Research Study 207. London: Research, Development, and Statistics Directorate, Home Office.

Wilson, Kenneth L. and Alejandro Portes. 1980. "Immigrant Enclaves: An Analysis of the Labor Market Experiences of Cubans in Miami." *American Journal of Sociology* 86: 295-319.

Wilson, William J. 1987. *The Truly Disadvantaged.* Chicago: University of Chicago Press.

Wilson, William J. 1996. *When Work Disappears: The World of the New Urban Poor.* New York: Random House Press.

Wirth, Louis. 1938. "Urbanism as a Way of Life." *American Journal of Sociology* 44:1-24.

Zhang, Pidi and Jimi Sanders. 1999. "Extended Stratification: Immigrant and Native Differences in Individual and Family Labor." *The Sociological Quarterly* 40: 681-704.

Zhou, Min and Carl L. Bankston III. 1998. *Growing Up American: How Vietnamese Children Adapt to Life in the United States.* New York: Russell Sage Foundation Press.

Zhou, Min and Carl L. Bankston III. 2006. "Delinquency and Acculturation in the Twenty-First Century: A Decade's Change in a Vietnamese American Community." In *Immigration and Crime: Race, Ethnicity, and Violence* edited by Ramiro Martinez, Jr. and Abel Valenzuela, Jr. New York: New York University Press.

Index

Breinigsville, PA USA
02 March 2010
233432BV00002B/1/P